MY LETTERMEN YEARS:

THE JOURNEY TO HELL AND BACK

BY JIM PIKE
WITH E. L. SCOTT

iUniverse, Inc.
Bloomington

MY LETTERMEN YEARS:
THE JOURNEY TO HELL AND BACK

iUniverse books may be ordered through booksellers or by contacting:

iUniverse
1663 Liberty Drive
Bloomington, IN 47403
www.iuniverse.com
1-800-Authors (1-800-288-4677)

ISBN: 978-1-4759-4079-4 (sc)
ISBN: 978-1-4759-4080-0 (e)

Library of Congress Control Number: 2012915737

Printed in the United States of America

iUniverse rev. date: 9/5/2012

CONTENTS

FOREWORD

I first heard of Jim Pike when I was a young radio announcer—I only knew him as a singer and the founder of The Lettermen. A few years later, my wife and I fell in love to Jim's sounds of "When I Fall in Love"! Twenty years later, I was managing a radio station in Idaho Falls, Idaho, and we booked Reunion to do two shows—I have been a devoted fan since! In 1999, Jim and Reunion returned to Idaho Falls to do a few shows, and for the past thirteen years, I have had the pleasure to be part of producing and hosting dozens of shows for Reunion. Onstage or off—Jim Pike is a *class act!*

My wife and I have had the opportunity to become friends with Jim and Sue Pike. We have seen firsthand how their love of music has blessed many thousands of lives—including ours. Jim's story is inspirational and motivating! Jim Pike certainly has "Made It through the Rain"!

Mike Adams

♫♫♫

Winter quarter brought me together with Jim Pike. This changed the direction my life would take for the next few years. We were in the male chorus together, and when I formed a quartet, he was first in line to audition when I announced that I was putting together a quartet that would do Four Freshmen arrangements. I'll never forget our audition. He sang well out of the hymn book. Then I played a major seventh chord and asked him to find his part. He made a noise and said, "Am I high or low?" We still get a laugh out of that.

Buck Farley

♫♫♫

Jim Pike is a gifted man and a wonderful friend. He and I have spent many happy times together—singing, traveling, double-dating, and sharing ideas and beliefs. We appeared together on a TV episode of *Dobie Gillis*, which was a lot of laughs. Few people in my life have been as fun, as talented, and as reliable as my dear friend Jim Pike.

Sterling Brimley

♪♪♪

Music was Jim's life, and he worked hard at it. His mind was constantly at work, thinking about arrangements, songs to record, and who to see next to get a record deal. He did everything he could to develop his talent. The fear of losing his voice actually resulted in him losing the use of it, causing him to have to hire someone to take his place. Of course, Jim is much more than just a voice, which he has come to realize. However, Jim is a fighter and a very strong individual. With proper treatment, Jim eventually recovered and was able to use his wonderful talent again. Jim continues to do beautiful productions and vocal arrangements, which receive critical acclaim wherever he performs.

Bobby Engemann

♪♪♪

My first memories with my older brother, Jim, were in Salmon, Idaho. We lived just about a mile and a half from the Salmon River up on a bluff that was called the Bar. We lived in a modest home with our mother after her divorce from our dad. It was there that Jim taught me how to fish for trout; we still share that love today. Jim was my big brother, and I looked up to him. I still look up to him. Singing with him for all these years has been priceless! I love ya, Jim.

Gary Pike

♪♪♪

Jim Pike is one of a kind. I have had the privilege of knowing and singing with him for the past thirty years. He was blessed with incredible musical talents and used them to add beauty to this world. How many people can be transformed back in time by just hearing the beginning notes of one of his (The Lettermen's) hits? Millions!

With all of that talent and success, he has always stayed true to his religious beliefs. He is a wonderful husband and father. He is generous, kind, and gentle … we have cried together in more movies than I care to remember. And to top it off, he is one heck of a fisherman! I love Jim Pike.

Ric de Azevedo

♪♪♪

I have a few words I would like to share. We all know of the many accolades given to Jim Pike, The Lettermen, and Reunion. Jim has received comments and/or letters from Frank Sinatra, President George W. Bush, Senator Orrin Hatch, Governor Herbert, Governor Kempthorne, Jack Benny, George Burns, Johnny Carson, President Gordon B. Hinckley of the LDS Church, and many, many more from all over the world. While these wonderful words of praise are touching, I wanted to acknowledge the man I've been married to for forty-three years.

Jim is a complex man. He is tenacious, strong, boyish, loving, tender, compassionate, honest, talented, God-loving, and just about the best husband and father anyone could ask for. I met Jim right around the time The Lettermen were at the peak of their career.

When we met, he had his mother, sister, and brothers living with him. He wanted to give them a better life. What a wonderful attribute. I was visiting Jim and his family one weekend when he put the medley together "Goin' Out of My Head/Can't Take My Eyes Off of You." He was sunning out by his pool and came running into the house to share his idea and quickly write it down. He was like a little kid! While we were on tour, he used to twirl the knob on the radio to hear what was playing to get ideas. It drove me nuts. We kept a log in the glove box to jot down all of his ideas. It was that free spirit and wonder that I fell in love with.

As I look back and see how he met his challenges head-on, seeking the help that he needed to survive, and working so hard to attain true happiness, I have the deepest admiration and respect for him. After all these years, I am joyful that his story is finally being told. Each year I love him more. We are blessed with our faith, our wonderful marriage, and our very special daughter, Kelly.

Sue Pike

♪♪♪

ACKNOWLEDGMENTS

Thanks to the following:

Sue for being my partner and confidante.

Karl Engemann for our first Capitol Records contract.

Jess Rand for guiding the career of The Lettermen.

William Morris Agency for the thousands of college
concerts and nightclub appearances.

Ruth Sowby for getting this project off the ground.

Shela Hampton for being the glue that has held everything together.

E. L. Scott for her unwavering patience in
putting these stories on paper.

The many musicians who have played for us over the years,
helping us to be the best in person and on our recordings.
The loyalty and talents of Everett Reed, Blair Andersen, and
Mike Fleetwood, and our audio team of Harry and Steve
White for always being there and making us sound great.

Bobby, Gary, Ric, and Tony, thanks for the music and the memories.

PROLOGUE:
Goin' Out of My Head

Jim Pike—Lettermen Days

How the hell did I get here? I lay back in my hospital bed, closed my eyes, and tried to remember—Sue crying; the trips to Dr. Kardiner's office; one tranquilizer—no, two; eyes staring into my face; my darling wife, Sue, trying to hold me down to keep me from flopping all over the room as the pain of depression engulfed me. I opened my eyes, managed to throw the covers off and swing my feet over the bed, and then I froze.

There, in one of the corners of the room, was a man standing on his head with his Jockey shorts over his face. Repulsed, I shrunk back. *I don't belong here*, I thought. *I'm not crazy. I don't belong with these people.* I was in Edgemont Psychiatric Hospital—alone, confused, and not sure if I was ever going home.

My psychiatrist, Dr. Kardiner, had suggested I check myself into Edgemont. That way, when I felt ready, I could check myself back out. Dr. Kardiner had already given me two tranquilizers, but there was no noticeable improvement. Sue and I agreed I needed to get to the hospital. After waking up in that room though, I wanted to check out immediately.

The doctors let me call Sue at six o'clock that morning. I heard the worry in her voice when she answered. "Get me out of here," I begged her. "I'm in here with a bunch of loonies. I'm not loony." I didn't think I could survive in such a sterile and colorless atmosphere.

"Jim, let me call Dr. Kardiner, okay?" answered Sue. "I'll call him, and then I'll call you back." She called back within two minutes. "Dr. Kardiner wants you to stay there, but I'm getting dressed right now, and I'm on my way."

Sue drove to Edgemont, and within an hour, she got me into a private room. Sue kept me hopeful that week. That first day, she brought crossword puzzles and a television with rabbit ears. None of the rooms had televisions in case the patients decided to use them to hurt themselves or others. Twice a day, Sue walked with me to therapy. We had to pass one hallway where we always heard people screaming in the rooms with padded walls. They were in those rooms for their own protection, but Sue and I couldn't help but shiver each time we passed by.

After five days of therapy, one of the doctors suggested Sue take me out to lunch. I told her okay, and since we were out, I needed a new pair of Levi's. We went to the Broadway Department Store at Hollywood and Vine to get a pair of jeans. Sue had just started pulling out a couple of pairs when I suddenly looked at her. I was frightened as I whispered, "Take me back."

CHAPTER 1:
Memories

I was born November 6, 1936, to Joy, an affectionate mother, and Russ, a famous cowboy singer.

My mom was very petite, only about four feet and eleven inches. She had these big, wide eyes that made her look like one of Walt Disney's rabbits, but she was absolutely beautiful. When I was in elementary school, I would bring the boys from my class home to see how pretty my mom was. I thought she was an angel. She was very fun-loving—she loved to laugh and had a great personality. Mom came from a large family, and all of our family had nicknamed her Joy because she was so happy. She had been schooled only until eighth grade, but she was a successful waitress. Mom always got big tips because everyone liked her.

My father was part of a group called Russ Pike and His Prairie Knights. They were pretty popular, especially in the Midwest, and traveled all over the country. Radio shows were my dad's thing; he

Jimmy Pike—Age 2

played on all the 50,000-watt radio stations. When I was three, he started taking me with him to do radio shows. After they rang the cowbell at the end of his show, I would sing, "There's an old prairie schooner, wending its way, over the Santa Fe 'Twail,'" while my mom and uncles sang the background pieces. After my first time, my dad smiled at me and said, "Jim, you've got to be the youngest singer to ever sing that song on the radio." When I turned four, my dad let me open each show with "God Bless America." There's still a recording of it in the Library of Congress.

I loved singing until my first time in front of a live audience at one of my dad's rodeos. I was about five. It wasn't the audience that scared me—I don't think I had stage fright—it was that microphone! I had no idea how powerful a microphone could make my voice sound. I can still recall the reverberation of my voice: my dad set me up on a chair in front of it, and when I went "Ga-a-a-a," the microphone went "GA-GA-GA-GA" back at me. It's funny now, but that moment scared me enough that I didn't want to sing anymore. I don't have another childhood memory of me singing.

"Happy" Jack, Jimmy Pike, Joy Pike (mother),
Russ Pike (father), unknown, Uncle Floyd (Josh) Pike

From the time I can remember, I was fearful of my dad. In 1945, I didn't see my dad for nearly six months. He'd moved to Oklahoma to work on WKY, a 50,000-watt radio station. When my mom and I moved there to join him, my dad met us at the train station. I remember standing up and thinking my dad had shrunk. He wasn't the big man he used to be when I was scared of him as a little boy.

This is how Jimmie (mascot of the Prairie Knights) looks now, sure growing isn't he?

Jimmy Pike

On my first day of school in Oklahoma, the teacher asked me to introduce myself. I didn't want to just be "Jim." When I was younger, I wanted to be anyone but Jim, so I told the class my name was Rusty. I liked that name, and I was sure the other kids would like me because of it. Of course, being "Rusty" didn't get anyone to like me; in fact, I got teased because I hadn't given my real name. I didn't realize it then, but this was my first time trying to be what I believed others wanted in order to be liked. It's taken me years to be happy with who I am.

I remember going to California from the Midwest for the first time. We moved there after a Beverly Hills agency sent talent scouts to see my dad at one of the rodeos. He and his backup band, comprising my mom and uncles, were very popular. At the rodeo, my dad always wore his white hat because he said it made him "the good guy." He twirled a rope and had a pair of pistols he flashed at the crowd while doing his rope tricks. The audience loved him, but I've always thought Boots, his horse, stole the show. Always standing tall and strong, Boots could count with his hooves, answer "yes" and "no" questions with a specific whinny, and sure did know how to take a bow when the audience applauded him. Boots knew he was something special. I treasured that horse and used to ride him almost every day out in the pasture.

When the scouts from the Beverly Hills agency had seen my dad's show and noticed Boots with his silver saddle, they brought our family out to California. Republic Pictures wasn't well known, but they wanted my dad to make movies for them as a singing cowboy. B Westerns is what they called those movies—where the good guy never gets his hat knocked off. My dad said it was the silliest thing he'd ever heard of. He considered himself a true cowboy—I'd seen him shoot a jackrabbit from his horse with a nice clean shot—so he turned them down. About a month later, they signed on this guy named Gene Autry. Go figure!

After California, we moved to Twin Falls, Idaho. Dad went to work for Bud Larson, or "Big Bud" as everyone called him. Big Bud was about seven feet tall and looked like James Arness. Dad's job was to herd Bud's cattle and brand them. Dad was still singing on the radio at the time, and kids at school teased me because of it. I realize now they were probably just jealous, but back then it was enough for me to tell my dad I didn't want to sing anymore.

"You're not going to sing anymore? Ever?"

I looked down at my feet and answered him, "No, sir."

Dad just shook his head and walked out of the room. Later that day, he came up to me and said if I didn't want to sing, I didn't have to. Years later, that moment still means a lot to me. I don't have many memories of my father being as understanding of me as he was that day. For the most part, my dad tended to be mean. He never hit me or anything, but he would yell a lot, especially at my mother.

I remember my mother coming into my bedroom one day when I was around seven years old to ask, "How would you like to have a little brother?" I jumped up, yelled "Yes!" and pumped my fists into the air. A few months later, Gary was born. By the time Gary came along, our dad had mellowed a lot, so Gary knew a different father than I did. Sometimes I would tell Gary about how hard Dad had pushed me or how he would tell me I'd never amount to anything. Dad was from the old school, so he was always trying to put me down, thinking that would force me to make something of myself. Gary would get this confused look on his face and say, "I don't remember Dad like that at all."

Home for me was never one place, especially after my parents' divorce. I was constantly moving from Missouri to Oklahoma, to California, to Idaho, and then back to California. My parents divorced in 1946 while we were living in Twin Falls, Idaho. Mom got remarried to a man named Don Unangst and settled in Salmon, Idaho. Dad went to Idaho Falls with his new wife, Gerri. Gary and I stayed with Dad and Gerri for a while, and I remember going to O. E. Bell Junior High in Idaho Falls for a short time. Then Gary and I moved in with our mom, where I attended Salmon High School. It was frustrating constantly switching back and forth between the two of them. It wasn't until high school that I remained at the same school for more than three months; I attended Idaho Falls High School for three years.

For most of junior high, I lived with my mom in Salmon, Idaho. I was grateful when I moved in with her because I was finally going to a school where no one knew my dad was Russ Pike from the radio. I was at a vulnerable age, and my self-esteem was pretty low. I'd never stayed in one school for very long, so I never had any success at making friends. I was always the new kid in town. In junior high, I got into sports, mainly football and baseball. Singing continued to fade into the background. The world of sports was something that allowed me to fit in.

I was prepared to play baseball because I had played Little League for a while in Twin Falls, and my dad had taught me how to throw a curveball. Nobody knew what a curveball was back in those days in Idaho. One time I struck out nineteen batters just because I could throw a curveball, but my dad stopped coming to my games. He couldn't play Minor League baseball anymore because of his arm, so he gave up on the game and threw away everything that had to do with baseball—including my Little League games.

Song and Picture Book (Prairie Knights)

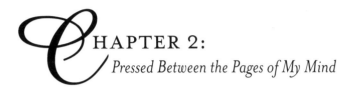

CHAPTER 2:
Pressed Between the Pages of My Mind

In my freshman year of high school, I went out for the football team. I played sports so that I could fit in and be part of a team, but football initiation was rough in that little Idaho town. The players blindfolded us new guys and made us eat what we thought were worms. In reality, it was only spaghetti. Another time they took sardines, tied a thread around their heads, dipped them in Hershey's chocolate, and then made us swallow them whole. When we had done it, they yanked them back up. It was horrible! Once I had to walk downtown with the rest of the freshmen players wearing hip waders, a woman's skirt, two grapefruits stuck in my shirt, and Limburger cheese rubbed through my hair. The stench of the cheese was overwhelming as we marched down the street single file, but I was willing to go through initiation because I wanted to belong. I wanted the other team members to like me.

I finally started singing again when I joined the choir at my high school. By this time, I was back in Idaho Falls with my dad. I discovered singing wasn't so bad when I was in a group. No one made fun of me or paid much attention to me because I blended in with the rest of the boys. I wouldn't sing solos in front of people who knew me, but I did decide to give solo singing a try at out-of-town competitions, which were usually about twenty miles from home. At these music contests, the judges would grade you A, B, C, or D—A being the best score. I would pick a classical piece to sing, and I would always get an A and take first place in the solo category. Singing at these competitions helped remind me what I liked about music in the first place and how much I enjoyed singing. I didn't want to be known as Russ Pike's kid; I just wanted to sing.

In 1953, during eleventh grade at Idaho Falls High, I decided I was going to enter the talent show. My friends were in charge of putting the show together, and when I told them I wanted to enter, they gave me a hard time—gave me the horse laugh, if you will. "Oh, Jim, you don't sing." That's what they thought, but I knew I could do it. For the talent show, I rented a tux and white gloves, painted my face black, and performed like Al Jolson. Back then, Al Jolson was huge. The movie *The Jolson Story* had a soundtrack the kids in high school were crazy about. I was already doing Al Jolson impressions of "Rock-a-Bye Your Baby with a Dixie Melody" using my dad's recording equipment for fun. I decided to take a chance and perform it at the show. I got up to sing with no accompaniment, just a cappella. I was scared to death. I got a standing ovation though, and I won. My friends were both stunned and impressed. "Jim, you can sing!" Their support helped boost the confidence I would later need to pursue a singing career.

After that talent show, all the students at my school knew how good I was at singing. In my senior year, my classmates wanted me to be the singer for senior prom. I rehearsed with a band the class hired. I sauntered out on stage in a turquoise blue dinner jacket with the pants to match, and I sang like Perry Como—smooth and easy. Everyone seemed to have a good time. Still, being a professional singer wasn't in the picture. That had been my dad's thing. I had spent so many years trying to distance myself from The Prairie Knights, I didn't recognize that the desire to sing professionally was still inside of me.

Russ Pike and His Prairies Knights with Mascot Jimmy Pike

CHAPTER 3:
Bits and Pieces

I graduated from high school in May 1954, broke and unsure of what I wanted to do with my life. My friends were all going off to college, but I didn't have the money to join them. In the middle of July, I saw an article in the paper that said all the armed services were shutting down the GI Bill on August 1. I ran down and joined the navy so I could get the GI Bill that would make it possible for me to go to college eventually.

One of the things I absolutely disliked about boot camp was marching on the blacktop with a

Jim Pike, Navy Radar Man

rifle under the San Diego sun. Guys would pass out from the heat. When I got word the base was holding auditions for a navy choir, I signed up right away. I had a good ear and listened at the door of the auditions, so by the time it was my turn, I had the song memorized and made the choir. I loved being in the navy choir. I would sit by the window during practice, and when my company would march by, I'd smile and wave at them while they would all flip me the finger; it was all in good fun. I got put on easy duty and never had to march again under that sweltering sun.

After boot camp, I was assigned to a Landing Ship Tank (LST). Its job was to carry the marines and their small boats so they could land on the beaches. Many marines got sick the first few weeks out; some never got over their seasickness. I was on the deck force at the front of the ship. It was very cold. I spent three days on guard duty, standing on the bow at three in the morning with the freezing spray coming up, swabbing the deck, and getting blasted by the chilly ocean wind. I decided I'd had enough. I went up to the captain's quarters and knocked on his door. When he answered, his frame took up the entire doorway, and he said, "Yes, boy?"

Shaking slightly, I somehow found my voice and told him, "I want to go to school." I don't know where I got the courage to tell him that.

"Oh really?"

"Yes. Who's leaving the ship that I could replace? I don't care what position it is, I'll go to school for it."

He thought about it for a moment. "One of our radar men is leaving in a couple months. How would you like to go to radar school? You can take the correspondence course. I'll send for the books, and if you pass the test, you'll be my radar man."

I read and read and read as much as I could, whenever I had the chance. I had never been one to study much in high school, yet here I was, studying these books as if my life depended on it. I passed the test with a 95 percent score a few weeks after I first spoke to the captain, and within a matter of days, I was the radar man. The best part about being the radar man was that I got to sit in the warm con with the captain. My poor buddies were still swabbing away out front. My job as the radar man was to plot our course. And when we anchored, I would have to plot on the map where we were anchored, plot out two buildings on land, and put their coordinates in. Whoever was on watch had to check every hour to make sure none of those points had moved. If any of them had, that meant the ship wasn't properly anchored and was moving. Luckily, we never had that happen. Little did I know that determination to plot a course would stay with me for years to come.

I was in the navy for about a year when my knee got swollen from climbing the ladders. I had injured my knee when I was eight or nine years old. At that time, my parents were separated, and I was living in Cherokee, Iowa, with my mother's sister and her husband. It was Christmastime, and I was riding my bicycle on the slippery driveway when I fell off and bruised and twisted my knee. I got up and was walking just fine, so my aunt never thought to take me to a doctor. My knee never gave me any problems until later on when I was playing football. It would occasionally lock up on me and get stiff. I would sit out a game or two, and then I could go back and play for three to four months before it locked up again. When I first joined the navy, it was bothering me, and when they asked for anybody with a bad knee to step forward, I did. They had me sign a piece of paper and then step back in line. They still let me in, and I was fine in boot camp. It wasn't until I was climbing those ladders that my knee started acting up again.

Every day, my knee got worse and worse. Finally, Ensign Miller, a friend of mine from our ship's basketball team, suggested I go see the naval doctor, Dr. Stricker, in the naval hospital in Corona, California.

When I finally went to see Dr. Stricker, I had been in the navy for one year and one month. When Dr. Stricker saw my knee, he said it was so bad, he didn't want to operate on it and end up having to pay me disability.

"Tell you what," he said, "I'll give you a medical discharge, and you'll get a GI Bill for two years since you've been in a little over a year. How's that sound to you?" I was still just a kid, and I was homesick. The offer sounded pretty good to me, and I took the deal.

I arrived at Brigham Young University in the fall of 1955. It took three months for my GI Bill to catch up with me. I had only eleven dollars in my pocket, so I was allowed to sign up for classes and buy all my books on credit. Most nights, I played my guitar under the girls' dorm windows, and they'd throw me money and food. Other times, I pretended I was doing a scavenger hunt. I had a sheet with items listed on it, and I would have all but one crossed out. I'd knock on dorm room doors and tell the students in there all I needed was one more apple or a couple of eggs to win.

In high school, they had talked about career choices and how your IQ should match you up with the type of job you're qualified to do. I had an above-average IQ, but I had spent all my life fishing and being out in the woods, so I thought I wanted to be a forest ranger. I took the aptitude test with the rest of my high school psychology class. On certain things, I didn't even show on the graph, such as mechanical. I didn't show up on clerical either. But I did show up sky-high on science and outdoors, which made being a forest ranger make even more sense. However, after looking at the pay scale for a forest ranger, I went with geology. I thought if I was really good and studied really hard, I might be able to get on with an oil company or even find my own oil if I was really industrious. So I entered BYU with the intention of majoring in geology and getting a minor in music.

I decided to minor, rather than major, in music. Most people who major in music and want to sing end up singing in Broadway shows. I didn't want that. I was singing pop music, and I wanted to focus on having a hit record. One teacher was head of the madrigal choir. When I was a couple of minutes late for a class, he turned to me and said, "Oh, I see that our crooner has finally arrived." That made me so mad, I turned to the rest of my class and said, in a big operatic voice, "Well, it's a hell of a lot better than singing, 'Praise Ye!'" The kids just screamed and laughed as I walked out on the professor and the class. A lot of the music teachers were like that though. I was a guy who really wanted to make it in show business, and they'd make fun of me.

Back in high school, everyone who signed my yearbook said I should sing professionally. So when I entered BYU, I decided to seek out Janie Thompson, the program director for the school. Janie would gather together this big group of performers and would travel all over the country with them while they sang at different high schools. Janie was really talented at putting vocal groups together and devoted her life to helping students learn to perform. Janie called her program the "Student Program Bureau." When I went to see her, I told her I was interested in singing, and she had me come in the next day to audition.

When I got there, she said, "What do you want to sing?"

"Sinatra's 'What's New.'"

"All right." She sat down at the piano and started playing.

I sang, "What's new? How is the world treating you?" Janie stopped playing the piano and started crying.

When she was finally able to look up from her lap, she said, "Jim, you are going to be a big star someday." Needless to say, I sang with Janie's Student Program Bureau for a while.

The Y's Men was the number-one jazz band out of all the colleges in the nation—they were tops! I was at a dance of theirs one evening. I went up to the bandstand and asked Dick Balleu, who was the bandleader, if I could sing "Love Is a Many Splendored Thing" with them. He said yes, and after he heard me sing, Dick asked me, "How would you like to sing with the band permanently?"

"With you guys? You mean it? I'd love that!" I was on my way to being a soloist with The Y's Men when I walked into the Cougar Eat on a cool autumn afternoon and my life changed.

CHAPTER 4:
And I Think to Myself

The Cougar Eat was a small cafeteria on the BYU campus that held about a hundred people. It had a jukebox, a soda fountain, and all the cheeseburgers you wanted. When I heard *"And when I held her in my arms, my heart felt warm"* start playing on the jukebox, that was it; my dreams of solo singing were out of the picture.

"Who's that group? Who's that group?" I started shouting.

"Well that's 'It Happened Once Before' by The Four Freshmen. They're the new rage."

Four Freshmen: Hal Kratzsch, Don Barbour, Bob Flanigan, Ross Barbour

I wanted to break open that jukebox and eat the record—just take that forty-five and consume it. Singing in a group had never appealed to me before. I wanted to be the next Frank Sinatra, but when I heard that harmony, I thought, "Now *that's* group singing; that's what I want to do." I had never heard anything like that song. I knew I had to make music that sounded just like that.

Soon after I had heard this new sound, a guy named Buck Farley announced to the male chorus group that he wanted to start a quartet. I didn't pay much attention to him until he said, "A group that's gonna sound like The Four Freshmen." At those words, I practically climbed over the backs of the other students to audition for his group. When I tried out later that day, I hit the note Buck played and then turned to him and asked, "Am I high or low?" We became best friends right away.

One of the first groups we put together was called The Nomads. When we started out, I was singing bass, Buck was singing baritone, and even though our high tenor and second tenor were mediocre, we still thought we had a good group. One day, while walking on campus, Buck and I passed a rehearsal studio and heard this beautiful singing, just like harmonies we sang. Buck and I looked at each other, and we couldn't help ourselves; we opened the door. Inside there was a group of five guys who all sounded really good, much better than our group. The high tenor sounded just like Bob Flanigan of The Four Freshmen. We hung around until they were finished with their rehearsal, and then we took their high tenor and bass aside and asked if they would sing with us. And man, there it was. Noel Burke was singing the high tenor, Buck went up to second tenor, I was at baritone where I belonged, and Ron Vaughn became our bass singer. With the new group, we changed our name from The Nomads to The Damons—we came up with that name by spelling *Nomad* backward. The Damons' first gig was singing at the BYU homecoming. When we sang those harmonies together, I would just cry. They were so beautiful, I'd tear up and wouldn't be able to continue singing. It did something to me, and my solo career was gone for good.

The Damons started with Buck, Noel, Ron, and me, but then Noel began having trouble with his first wife. She wanted him to go to school and stop hanging out with us "buckaroos" and singing. Actually, she didn't want him to have anything to do with show business at all. She happened to be sick at the time and wanted him home more often. I could understand that. I can remember going over to their house, and she would literally cling to him to stop him from going out with us. Eventually, Noel quit, and Glenda Farish took his place.

Damons: (top) Buck Farley, Jim Pike, Noel Burke, Ron Vaughn

I had become acquainted with Glenda through doing tours with Janie Thompson while Glenda was singing with a group called The Esquires. I thought she was a great group singer. She had a fabulous voice and was good looking; she looked like Donna Reed. The Damons were in Los Angeles at the time, and I knew Glenda was living in California, so I called her.

"Glenda, it's Jim Pike. How'd you like to sing with The Damons? We'll be singing harmonies like The Four Freshmen."

"Oh I'd love that," she said. "I love The Four Freshmen."

Glenda was with us for about a year but left when she started having problems with her husband. In the meantime, Ron had married Bonnie, a cute blonde from a group called Three Dolls who came up to BYU to sing, and Bonnie took Glenda's place.

Early on, when it was still Noel, Buck, Ron, and me, The Damons auditioned for a 1950s talent show on TV called *Rocket to Stardom,* hosted by Bob Yeakel. It was an eighteen-hour-long weekly talent show that played from Saturday afternoon to Sunday. Think *American Idol*, only you never quite knew what was going to happen because it was live television. We made it on the show and won first place with the song "It's a Blue World" by The Four Freshmen. After that, we immediately got a call from Atlanta Records in Hollywood. They wanted to meet us and asked how soon we could come to their studio. When we met with them, they gave us some material, and we signed a record contract. Just like that. One song on *Rocket to Stardom*, and we had a contract with a big-time record company. They gave us four songs to learn, one of which was called "Dreamy Eyes." We took them home and rehearsed. We liked "Dreamy Eyes" the best, but not how it sounded. It was too doo-wop, so we changed the piece to the harmonies we had been singing, The Four Freshmen harmonies. When we took our demo back to Atlanta Records, they told us we couldn't sound like that. We had to sound doo-wop because "that's what sells." We tore up the contract. Was it a mistake? I don't know. But we were young, knew what we wanted, and weren't willing to change our style to "go commercial."

The Damons' next big audition was for Stan Kenton. He was the one who had given The Four Freshmen their start, and he flipped when he heard us. Glenda was with us by this time, and we were invited to audition for a television show he was starting on Balboa Island in California. It had the big Stan Kenton orchestra, and it was incredible! This was during the summer of 1958, and we weren't currently in school. Stan Kenton had six different television shows, and we sang on every one. Singing with him really opened a lot of doors because it got our names out there. People on the street actually recognized me and would say, "Hey, aren't you one of The Damons?"

Those months on Kenton's shows were awesome—we were singing, and we were creating a name for ourselves. I'll never forget the first time someone knew my name. We were still a part of the Stan Kenton group and went to see Stan and The Four Freshmen at the Palladium Ballroom in Hollywood. While we were watching the show, a man came up to me. He was a tall half-Mexican, half-Apache and was staring right at me as if I were a star. He started shaking, could hardly swallow, and asked, "Are you Jim Pike of The Damons?" I was stunned. He said it like I was some big deal. I didn't consider myself anything special, and I was blown away by his demeanor. This man was Connie Figueroa, who would later take Buck's place in The Damons.

It was Stan Kenton who first noticed the lump on Buck's neck. Buck hadn't been feeling well but blew it off as the stress of doing the shows. When Stan saw the lump on his neck though, he wanted Buck to get it checked out right away. Turned out it was Hodgkin's disease. Buck ended up going to Maryland to Johns Hopkins University. It was the leading hospital at the time, and the doctors there said he had only two years to live. We all prayed for him the night before his surgery. The next day, when they went to do his surgery, they couldn't find the cancer. Forget about two years; Buck lived more than forty years past that scheduled surgery.

When Buck left, we held auditions for baritones, and I ended up singing second. It was a bit out of my range, but I could do it. That's when I found out Connie Figueroa could sing second tenor. We met up on the BYU campus on Saturday afternoon.

"I've been group singing for years," said Connie.

"Really? What part do you sing?"

"Second tenor."

"Oh yeah?"

"Yeah. Why?"

I grinned at him, tugged his arm, and told him to follow me to one of BYU's studio rooms. Connie auditioned and became The Damons' second tenor. I was content because I was back to baritone.

The Damons had a few releases with Warner Brothers Records but no hits. One was called "I'd Be a Fool," and Ron, Bonnie, and Connie sang the background for me. I released "Luci D," which had a folk-song sound to it, and Bonnie had a short solo in the middle of the song. I also recorded "Scarlet Ribbons," which made a bit of noise, but I was longing for us to have a hit song. To be on top.

After Connie joined the group, we had a chance at success when we got a phone call from Yvonne De Carlo. Yvonne De Carlo had the most beautiful exotic face and figure, and boy, could she dance. I fell in love with her when I was six, the first time I saw her as Cobra Woman. She called us because she had started singing, was going out for a forty-two-week tour, and wanted to hire us to be her background group. Up until this point, we hadn't had a paying gig, but Bonnie turned to me and said, "I can't do that. I'm married. I can't go out on the road."

I blew up at her and said, "Then what the heck have we been rehearsing for two years for? To go out on the road and make money! Now a job comes along, and you won't go?" It made me so upset she wasn't willing to go out on the road, I quit the group. Connie left too.

Years later, after The Lettermen had become successful, Connie became our bass player. After leaving The Lettermen, he became a famous jazz bass player. Ron ended up going to school in Pasadena, graduated at the top of his class, and became a chiropractor, with Bonnie working as his nurse. Noel went to Oregon and became a brick mason. Buck went to work for IBM. I went back to BYU that fall, and that's when Bobby Engemann and I put our voices together.

CHAPTER 5:
What a Wonderful World

I was in The Damons when I first met Bobby Engemann. Bobby was in a group called The Engemann Trio, whose claim to fame was being on *The Lawrence Welk Show*. Their group consisted of Bobby, his brother Karl, and Karl's wife, Gerri.

Karl Engemann, Gerri Engemann, Bobby Engemann

The Engemann Trio was singing a more traditional style with vibrato—commercial stuff—but Bobby had a beautiful, straight tone. He could sing lead and harmony—and I wanted to sing with him. One time, while The Damons were rehearsing for BYU's homecoming, Noel couldn't make it to a rehearsal. I saw Bobby walking by, so I hollered out, "Hey, Bobby! We're missing a guy! Come and sing with us!" Bobby came over and sang with Buck, Ron, and me. It sounded great. After that, we became close friends.

Bobby and I both had good solo voices, but I wanted to put them together. However, like most plans, there were a couple of glitches. For one, even though The Damons broke it off, I had to keep singing, and since I wasn't in a group, I ended up singing solos on the BYU Variety Show tours again. However, Bobby and I did end up going to California to try to make it as a duo like Simon and Garfunkel or The Righteous Brothers. We were getting ready to make some noise, maybe even get a record contract, when Bobby got a telegram from the Air National Guard that required him to report for active duty for seven months.

When Bobby left, I auditioned for a Las Vegas lounge group called Bill Norvis and the Upstarts. Bill's claim to fame was "Make Love to Me," which he wrote for Jo Stafford, and it was a big hit. His group was made up of two guys and two gals, but one of the guys in Bill's group, Gary Clark, was leaving for an acting role on *The Virginian*. When I got to the audition on Hollywood Boulevard, there were over one hundred guys waiting in line. I really didn't want to wait in that line. I had met Bill before, and he knew my voice, so I found the number of the rehearsal studio and called him. Lucky for me, he said to come on up. When I auditioned for him, I sang Frank Sinatra's "What's New" with all his phrasing and knocked Bill out! The two girls in the group started swooning while the other guy in the group, Tony Butala, stood behind them.

I made the group, and we started doing the Vegas tour. We sang mostly in lounges, but the group did not sound good. I kept telling Tony, "This group isn't gonna go." Every time Tony or I stepped up to sing a solo, we'd get a roaring applause. However, with the rest of the group, it wasn't working. The girls were great dancers and were built for Vegas, but they couldn't sing. And even though we were getting paid, Tony and I knew it wasn't going to last. I told Tony about Bobby because it was almost time for Bobby to come home. When we finished our tour, we both quit, causing Bill to hold auditions for another two guys. By this time, Tony and I had become fast friends. We went fishing together, double-dated, and just hung out.

When I dreamed about what I wanted my group to be like, the sound I wanted was similar to Glenn Miller's. I knew it had to be different, and I knew I wanted it to be three good-looking guys who could all sing solos and harmonies. It was the variety I wanted; that's what was going to get us on the map. Bobby was a good-looking guy. He reminded me a bit of Hugh O'Brian with his dark hair and thick, dark eyebrows. Then when I met Tony and heard his voice, I thought he would work well with Bobby and me. I even went as far as to ask Bobby once if he'd dye his hair red; that way, we would have a brunet, a blond, and a redhead. Almost like *Charlie's Angels*, before there was a *Charlie's Angels*. Of course, Bobby didn't dye his hair, but it was a fun thought.

CHAPTER 6:
Fools Rush In

When Bobby came home at the end of 1958, I introduced him to Tony, and we tried singing "Love Is a Many Splendored Thing." I used my guitar and taught them the chords to the song right then and there. I gave Tony the high part, Bobby the melody, and I sang the bass piece. When we hit that first chord on "love," we knew that was it; we were going to make it. We looked at each other and fell down laughing. We had it! We decided we would sing in three-part harmonies with real straight voices and straight harmonies. "It'll be different," Bobby said, "but I know it will go."

Now all we needed was a record contract. I was listening to the B side of Jimmie Rodgers's "Honeycomb" when I heard "Their Hearts Were Full of Spring." I chose that song and a song called "When" that a friend of mine had written. It was very much in the style of "Love Is a Many Splendored Thing" with big harmonies. That went on the B side of our demo. I put up money I had saved working as a mailman, did the vocal arrangements, and produced the session.

It takes a lot of work to produce a song. It would be nice if all we had to do was get up and sing, but I always wanted to be completely involved with my music. I wasn't going to let someone else make all the producing decisions. Our names were on the line, and I wanted us to succeed. For both "Their Hearts Were Full of Spring" and "When," I went to Gold Star Recording Studios in Hollywood on Hollywood and Vine. Tons of hits had come out of that recording studio. The studio had a celesta. The celesta sounds high like a harp, not harsh, but mellow like bells, which was the type of sound I was going for. A friend of mine played keyboards, and Jim Blaine was kind enough to play bass for us. We dubbed the song, which means that first we sang our three parts, and then, on another channel, we sang those same three parts over the original recording. That way, there were two voices singing each part, which gave the song a real haunting sound.

When we went to record the songs, I put the harmonies together, and we stayed until everyone had it memorized. I liked the way the songs turned out. They weren't masters, they were still only demos, but they were fresh and different. They had charm.

We took our demo recordings to Warner Brothers Records, and when they heard them, they signed us to the label immediately. This was an incredible blessing for us. Exactly two weeks from the moment we hit our first note together, we had a record contract! Warner Brothers wanted to test "Their Hearts Were Full of Spring" in their best test market—San Francisco. If it was big there, then they would release it nationally. "Their Hearts Were Full of Spring" *was* a big hit in San Francisco. It was the number-one record on the big rock station! The station said it went up to number one in a week. People were going wild over it.

Bobby and I were singing for homecoming at BYU when Don Graham, the national promotion man for Warner Brothers, called us and said, "Get here quick. You have a number-one record in the San Francisco market. The DJs want interviews!" We couldn't believe it. Bobby and I caught the next flight out of Utah to San Francisco, and Tony met us there.

One DJ who interviewed us was Gary Owens; this was before he became famous. The three of us sat down at the table with him, and he said, "Well, hello, boys, nice to meet you." He spoke with this big radio-sounding voice. We thought he was putting on a show for us, but then we found out it was his genuine voice. He actually spoke like that. Sitting in those interviews and talking to the DJs, I knew that this was the group that could make it—The Lettermen—Jim, Bobby, and Tony. After our interviews with the radio stations in San Francisco, we went back to Hollywood and met with the A&R (Artists and Repertoire) representatives from Warner Brothers. They told us they were not going to release the record nationally. We were stunned and disappointed. They told us, "We've got this guy Scottie Turnbull, who's a promising, young, up-and-coming songwriter to write four songs for you, and we're going to get you to record them."

A few days later, they brought us in at the end of a Joanie Sommers recording session. We had only fifteen minutes to record the music tracks and vocals for those songs. None of those songs were hit material though, and none of them made any noise. We decided we wanted out of our contract.

HAPTER 7:
The Way You Look Tonight

A t the time, Bobby's older brother, Karl, was a producer at Capitol Records. He set up a meeting for us with Nick Venet, a new, young record producer at Capitol. We met in a roomy office on the third floor of Capitol's building. Nick was very quiet while he listened to Karl's proposal and only nodded his head a couple of times. After Karl was done, Nick clapped his hands together, looked at us, and said, "Let's do it."

Karl was a lifesaver. Not only did he get us the interview with Capitol, he also called Warner Brothers and got us out

THE LETTERMEN

Jimmy Pike, Bobby Engemann, Tony Butala

of the contract we had with them. When we went over to Capitol, I didn't play any of the four songs we did with Warner Brothers. I knew Capitol wouldn't let us anywhere near the property, let alone in the door, with that noise. I gave them our original demo of "Their Hearts Were Full of Spring," the same one I had given Warner Brothers. Capitol loved it but told us they weren't going to release it nationally. Capitol wanted us to record four songs for them. This time though, we got to choose the songs we wanted to record.

At Capitol, we recorded "That's My Desire" and "The Way You Look Tonight." The former was on the A side of the record, but it died pretty quickly. Then one night, a disc jockey for the hottest rock station in Buffalo, New York, flipped the record to the B side and played "The Way You Look Tonight." Right away, the phones started ringing at the radio station with people asking about the song. The DJ called Hollywood to tell Capitol how popular the song was, and they said, "No. We don't want you to play the B side, we want you to play the A side. We're trying to push 'That's My Desire' over the hump." The next night, the same thing happened. The DJ played the A side with no response. As soon as he played the B side, the phones lit up. Again, he called Capitol to let them know, but they told him flat out, "No." This happened three nights in a row with the same results. The DJ called Capitol again and told them rather forcefully that the B side was the song that was going to make it. Finally, Capitol agreed. It's a good thing they did because "The Way You Look Tonight" made it to number thirteen in the nation practically overnight. It was August 1961, and we had our first hit.

After the record became a hit, we walked into the conference room at Capitol with our chests puffed out and our heads held high. Voyle Gilmore, the head of A&R at the time, looked at us and said, "You boys ain't nothing." You could see the air go out of our three bodies like three balloons being popped. But Gilmore kept us grounded. He said, "Right now, all you are is a one-hit wonder. If you have two more hits, and all three of those hits make it onto your first album, then you'll be up there with the big boys." Gilmore's words really made me think. I could have walked out of that meeting and picked any old standard, but I didn't want to be a one-hit wonder, so I thought hard about the songs I chose.

When we chose to record songs, we added harmonies but kept the original arrangements that had been a hit. People liked hearing the songs the way they originally came out. They didn't like it when we tried to change the arrangements. At the time, none of us were songwriters, so we didn't write any of our songs; instead, we redid a lot of old standards.

After our first hit record, we did a lot of college and high school performances with the Laundry List Shows, which comprised twenty musical groups that had current hit records. Every time The Lettermen

(top to bottom) Tony Butala, Jimmy Pike, Bobby Engemann

were announced, every girl would leave her boyfriend and come up to the front of the stage. They didn't want to dance to our song; they wanted to listen. They'd stand there and cry—we were their cry group; "... *and a laugh that wrinkles your nose touches my foolish heart*" were beautiful lyrics from "The Way You Look Tonight."

We really researched what our next single would be. I had this Nat King Cole album called *Stardust*, which was one of my favorite albums. I loved listening to it. It started off with this gorgeous orchestra, and at the end of the album, he'd sing, "*Sometimes I wonder why ...*" One night I was lying in bed listening to that album. "When I Fall in Love" came on, and I knew that was the song; that was our next hit. It was magical to listen to, and it still brings tears to my eyes when I listen to that album. "When I Fall in Love" did end up being our second hit when it reached number seven on *Billboard*'s Top 10 in 1961. It was even bigger than our first hit. Right then, we knew we weren't going to be a one-hit wonder group.

In 1962, Cynthia and Barry Mann wrote a song called "Come Back Silly Girl" with a piano theme. It had good harmony and was just contemporary enough that I gave in and took a chance on it. It didn't get as high as our first two hits, but when "Come Back Silly Girl" reached number seventeen, we had three hit singles in a row! Capitol decided to put out an album with all three hits on it, and the album became a gold record. The trick to making a hit album is that all the songs on the album must be great. I always tell young artists, "You can't put on three hit singles and nine songs to act as fillers and expect your album to make any noise." Every song on our album was a hit, so the album was great. That album went crazy and broke all kinds of records; we felt as if we were on the top of the world, and for a while, we were.

Something I've been asked quite often over the years is, "What makes a lead singer?" The question really isn't that simple to answer. Literally, the lead singer is the one in the band who sings the melody, but in The Lettermen, we all took turns singing the lead. For example, in "The Way You Look Tonight," we all took turns singing the melody and lead part, so when someone listens to it, it's hard to figure out who is singing which part at what time. We all wanted our group to be successful, and we all worked hard at making The Lettermen a success. I put my heart and soul into every song and every single chord. I did the research behind each song, and I arranged the harmonies. The Lettermen was my baby; it meant everything to me. Questioning who the lead singer was wasn't an issue back in '61. We were young, and our group was working its way to the top—we didn't have a care in the world.

When The Lettermen first started recording for Capitol, Glen Campbell was one of Capitol's top studio musicians. He played acoustic guitar on nearly every record. Glen had a few albums out himself, but they hadn't made much noise. Glen and I often talked after recording sessions, and I got to know him rather well. He was one of the most memorable people I've worked with. Glen told me he loved group singing, and for a short time, he was interested in joining The Lettermen. We had him sing with us on a few songs where we needed a fourth part, but before we decided whether to have a fourth member permanently, Glen had his hit, "By the Time I Get to Phoenix," and he was off.

It was also neat getting to work with men like George Burns and Jack Benny. One night early on in our career, we met George Burns at the Crescendo, an old nightclub down on the Sunset Strip that eventually became the Playboy Club. We discussed going out on tour with him. Burns was very quick-witted and funny, even offstage. He always had everyone laughing. He was famous for making new artists famous, such as Carol Channing and Ann-Margret. After we went out with George Burns, Jack Benny had to have us do his tour with him. It was the exact same tour as George Burns, so we did the same tour back-to-back. After that, Jack also had us on his television show.

During the next few years, we released some of our most popular songs. We had the medley of "Goin' Out of My Head/Can't Take My Eyes Off of You" and other songs, such as "Theme from a Summer Place," "Hurt So Bad," "Put Your Head on My Shoulder," and "Shangri-La." We started going out on the road and doing college concert tours. Our career took off—hit after hit. We did tours for about a twelve-year span—September 1961 through December 1973—during which time we did thousands of concerts and hundreds of television shows.

The Lettermen
America's Top Campus Trio!

DEBUT DATE	PEAK POS	WKS CHR	G O L D	ARTIST — Record Title	POP POS	Label & Number
★★33★★				**LETTERMEN, The**		
				Harmonic vocal group formed in Los Angeles in 1960. Consisted of Tony Butala (b: 11/20/40), Jim Pike (b: 11/6/36) and Bob Engemann (b: 2/19/36). First recorded for Warner Bros. Engemann replaced by Gary Pike (Jim's brother) in 1968.		
				1)When I Fall In Love 2)Hurt So Bad 3)Goin' Out Of My Head/Can't Take My Eyes Off You 4)Theme From "A Summer Place" 5)The Way You Look Tonight		
10/2/61	3	9		1 The Way You Look Tonight	13	Capitol 4586
				#1 hit for Fred Astaire in 1936		
11/27/61	1¹	13		2 When I Fall In Love	7	Capitol 4658
				#20 hit for Doris Day in 1952		
2/17/62	3	11		3 Come Back Silly Girl	17	Capitol 4699
5/19/62	16	6		4 How Is Julie?	42	Capitol 4746
8/19/65	2¹	12		5 Theme From "A Summer Place"	16	Capitol 5437
				from the film A Summer Place starring Sandra Dee/Troy Donahue		
9/18/65	8	10		6 Secretly	64	Capitol 5499
12/11/65	24	8		7 Sweet September	114	Capitol 5544
6/4/66	4	10		8 I Only Have Eyes For You	72	Capitol 5649
				#2 hit for Ben Selvin in 1934		
10/29/66	8	9		9 Chanson D'Amour	112	Capitol 5749
				#6 Pop hit for Art & Dotty Todd in 1958		
1/14/67	18	8		10 Our Winter Love	72	Capitol 5813
5/27/67	17	9		11 Volare		Capitol 5913
				#1 Pop hit for Domenico Modugno in 1958		
12/23/67	2²	14		12 Goin' Out Of My Head/Can't Take My Eyes Off You	7	Capitol 2054
3/30/68	9	8		13 Sherry Don't Go	52	Capitol 2132
11/9/68	8	13		14 Put Your Head On My Shoulder	44	Capitol 2324
3/1/69	16	8		15 I Have Dreamed	129	Capitol 2414
				from the musical The King And I #91 Pop hit for Chad & Jeremy in 1965		
5/10/69	2³	24		16 Hurt So Bad	12	Capitol 2482
10/11/69	8	8		17 Shangri-La	64	Capitol 2643
12/20/69	3	12		18 Traces/Memories Medley	47	Capitol 2697
3/28/70	18	6		19 Hang On Sloopy	93	Capitol 2774
6/6/70	8	9		20 She Cried	73	Capitol 2820
10/24/70	17	4		21 Hey, Girl	104	Capitol 2938
				#10 Pop hit for Freddie Scott in 1963		
1/2/71	34	5		22 Morning Girl		Capitol 3006
				#17 Pop hit for Neon Philharmonic in 1969		
				The Lettermen Present JIM PIKE		
1/23/71	8	8		23 Everything Is Good About You	74	Capitol 3020
6/5/71	33	4		24 Feelings		Capitol 3096
10/9/71	8	10		25 Love	42	Capitol 3192
				written by John Lennon		
6/9/73	25	6		26 Summer Song		Capitol 3619
				#7 Pop hit for Chad & Jeremy in 1964		
7/27/74	31	9		27 Touch Me In The Morning/The Way We Were		Capitol 3912
				#1 Pop hits for Diana Ross in 1973 and for Barbra Streisand in 1974		
2/1/75	16	11		28 Eastward		Capitol 4005
6/28/75	28	7		29 You Are My Sunshine Girl		Capitol 4096

TOP ADULT CONTEMPORARY 1961-1975

Top 40 Hits 1961–1975
Compiled from Billboard *and* Cashbox *magazines*

CHAPTER 8:
Just the Right Sound

When Bobby and I asked Tony to join us, it was hard for us to choose a name. All of us loved The Four Freshmen, so we wanted a collegiate theme name, but we didn't think there were any left. There were Danny and the Juniors, The Four Freshmen, The Four Preps, and The Seniors. We couldn't think of any name that would stand out against that crowd. We were at our wits' end. Bobby remembered something: both of us had lettered in high school and still had our letter sweaters. He shouted, "Why don't we call ourselves The Lettermen?"

"Yes!" Tony said. "But Mike Barnett owns the name." Tony used to sing with Mike. Tony called him, "Do you own the name The Lettermen?"

"No," said Mike. "The name has never been registered. We used it as our name but not professionally."

"Good!" was Tony's answer, and he hung up on Mike. Tony turned to us. "We can call ourselves The Lettermen."

We smiled at each other and then registered our name right away.

The Lettermen had a soft unison sound. Our harmonies were always a full triad with no vibrato, which gave us a big sound with a perfect blend. We were three clean-cut, good-looking guys who were great soloists as well as group singers. A perfect combination!

When we performed at high schools, we borrowed the letter sweaters from that school. When we walked out onto their stage, we were in their letter sweaters. After that, we went on to wear the white sweaters with the powder blue L on them. When we had a couple of hit albums, we were

Jim Pike, Bob Engemann, Tony Butala

popular with the adults as well as the high school and college kids, so we started dressing a bit more sophisticated. When the Nehru fashion was popular, we wore Nehru jackets with scarves because that was the style. The jackets were made from fine, light wool that draped softly around us. When we finally shed the letter sweaters, I was into Andy Williams and his look, so we started wearing gray alpaca sweaters with bright red Ivy League button-down shirts underneath and black mohair suit pants with black boots. That was our new thing. When we started playing at nightclubs for the adults, we went with tuxedos and had beautiful navy, dark brown, and black tuxes with boots dyed to match.

There were some colleges that had a reputation of not being good audiences for any performers, or were considered "dead," but they were just conservative. Conservative worked for us though because they liked our kind of music and respected us. The Midwest, the South, and Florida were our forte because, back then at least, they were more conservative.

We also played at all the major hotels across the United States, including the Fairmont, the Waldorf Astoria, and the Palmer House in Chicago. We broke records in every place, and we actually shredded Peggy Lee's record at the Palmer House. We'd get hired during prom seasons, and since the high school kids and the adults loved us, there would be a sea of white jackets as everyone lined up around the building to come into the nightclubs. They actually had to turn kids away every time we played at these hotels.

These nightclubs were called "supper clubs," and they had a sense of elegance about them. Supper clubs looked the way the clubs did in movies from the thirties and forties. People would get dressed up because the fashion was black tie. The supper clubs were usually in big, sophisticated hotels and had full orchestras. People could go out to dine and get up to dance to the orchestra during their meal. After the dinner and dancing, the show with us singing would begin. It's a shame they don't exist anymore. The cost of dinner and a show was pretty stiff. When families started moving to the suburbs, it was too pricy for them to get babysitters and drive into the city. Soon it was an end to an era. Today people go the casinos in Las Vegas and Atlantic City, where they have performances but no dinners in the showroom. Things have changed, but I'm so happy to have been a part of that great time.

The first time we played at the Fairmont Hotel in San Francisco, I was excited because the Venetian Room was such a sophisticated place. The

Fairmont was located on Knob Hill. It was beautiful, and right across the street was the Mark Hopkins Hotel. The outside of the hotel had a gothic architecture look. When you walked inside, there was plush burgundy carpeting and velvet furniture. Velvet drapes ran across the stage, and the giant marble pillars reminded me of the Coliseum in Rome. When guests walked through the doorway of the Venetian Room, the maître d' escorted them to their seat. We broke all the attendance records at the Fairmont, even Tony Bennett's, and that was his town because he had the hit "I Left My Heart in San Francisco."

The Fairmont is also special to me because that's the first place my wife, Sue, ever saw The Lettermen in concert. I met Sue on a blind date, and shortly thereafter, I invited her to the concert. I didn't want Sue to drive back to her apartment late at night by herself, so I suggested she bring one of her roommates. When Sue and her friend Carol got there, the place was packed. Hans, the maître d', told them to wait until the orchestra was finished playing the dance music, and then he would find a seat for them. Once the dance floor cleared, he brought out a table and two chairs and placed them on the edge of the middle of the dance floor. Hans then escorted the two ladies to their seats. When I got onstage, I looked down at Sue and smiled at her. She looked beautiful. Carol told Sue, "You're not only going out with the best-looking Letterman, but also with the one who has the best voice."

"I know," replied Sue. "I wasn't nervous before, but I am now!" Sue later told me that I seemed like just a normal guy when we were on our first date, but when she saw me onstage in my tux at the Fairmont Hotel, she knew I was something very special. I was a star.

The Lettermen were strictly a concert act, even in those supper clubs. No one got up and danced when we performed. When we played at the Fairmont for the first time, we were warned that the folks in San Francisco were so refined that there might not be much applause. If they liked us, there might be a polite applause. But the crowd went wild. They stood up on their chairs and clanged their spoons against their water glasses! Sue couldn't believe it. She had been to the Fairmont many times with her dad to see other performers, but her first time seeing The Lettermen in person was also her first time seeing this type of reaction at the Fairmont. The crowd loved us. It was in the papers too. The headline read something like "Lettermen knock 'em dead at the Fairmont Hotel."

The audience loved our kind of music. After that, we played at the Fairmont in September every year.

The Lettermen's season started in September at the Venetian Room at the Fairmont. We also played the Fairmont Hotel in Dallas, Texas, the Flamingo Hotel in Las Vegas, and then the Holiday House Supper Club in Monroeville, Pennsylvania, right before Christmas. After our Christmas break, we played the Blue Room at the Roosevelt Hotel in New Orleans, the Waldorf Astoria in New York City, and the Palmer House in Chicago. We also did a tour of more than two hundred colleges each year, often driving every day to a different college. Most of the club dates were for a duration of at least two weeks, so we loved being in the clubs. We could sleep in, turn in our laundry, get our cars serviced, get our hair cut, and shop. It was nice to feel grounded after doing a different city every day. But then, after doing two shows every night while at these supper clubs, we were ready again for the one-nighters.

Usually we played at the Palmer House in Chicago during the spring, but we were there one winter to play at the Auditorium Theatre. It was a big, old auditorium where they brought in all the current groups. Those were great audiences. During this winter trip, we brought our car to be serviced at the Cadillac dealership. Since our hotel was only eight blocks away, we figured we could walk it. But once we started walking, we didn't think we could make it past the first block. When we finally got back to the hotel, we found out that the temperature, with the wind chill, was forty-six degrees below zero! We had hats, gloves, heavy coats, and boots on, but no wonder we were still freezing. I promised myself I would never walk that far in the snow ever again.

The Blue Room in New Orleans was also fun to play, although I didn't like the great big pillars in the room. You'd walk down the steps and get a table. The stage was in front of the tables, but people had to look around the pillars to see the performers. I didn't care for that much, but our audiences were fine with it. They were great.

When we'd play in the Blue Room, there was this gal named Norma Jean who had a steady gig playing at the piano bar and singing. Sometimes Bobby and I stopped to listen to her sing on our way in or out of the hotel. Occasionally, we'd wait until Norma Jean was done for the night and then grab a seat to sit and talk with her. We hadn't known it, but Norma Jean had been watching us closely. One night she said, "You guys are different. Every entertainer who comes in here is always headed for the elevator with a different girl, but you guys come down by yourselves and go up by yourselves." That was the first moment I realized how much of what we were doing was being watched.

Thirty years later, Sue and I were attending church in Studio City, California, when Norma Jean walked in. We spoke with her after the meeting, and Norma Jean said she had been so impressed with our examples as clean-cut performers with morals that she wanted to know why we were so different. She investigated our church and became a member. I'm glad Bobby and I set good examples for her when we were performing at the Blue Room.

Vegas was also a great place to perform, and the audiences were fantastic for us. The Lettermen were busy all year round. When we weren't performing, we were recording for Capitol, but I loved every minute of it. Between recording, the supper clubs, the main rooms in Vegas, and the colleges, we kept ourselves busy.

We never tried to be "hip" because the minute we tried to be hip, we'd lose our audience. That's what always happens. It was best for us to stick with what we knew—our songs and dressing in black and navy tuxedos. If Sinatra never changed his style and went on as long as he did, then The Lettermen could last as well if we stuck with our original style. That way, we could have longevity.

CHAPTER 9:
You'll Never Walk Alone

Joy (mom), Gary (brother), Jim Pike

From the moment he could walk, my younger brother Gary was my shadow. As soon as Gary was old enough to tag along after me, he went with me every chance he had. My friends didn't want someone's little brother hanging out with us all the time, but I'd tell them, "If Gary doesn't go, I don't go." I always included Gary. We did everything together growing up, even fishing; we were fishing buddies. We also made sure we saw every movie that came out. There was never any rivalry or competition between us. Maybe it's because we're eight years apart, but we never felt the need to compete with each other.

When Gary was younger, he always amazed me because he never said anything unkind about anyone. He was like my mom in that way, very kind and caring. Everyone he met loved him—he reminded me of Beaver from *Leave It to Beaver*. Even after he joined The Lettermen, Gary would stand backstage, being polite and kind to all the fans. He's still the kind of guy people want to get to know.

I recall being very protective of Gary when he was younger. When my mom would change his diaper, and he'd look at me and start to roll over the edge of the sofa, I'd run over and push him back. My mom would've caught him in time, but I felt that, as his older brother, it was my job to be his protector. I think I was trying to be the father to him that I wanted my father to be to me—loving, supportive, and protective.

Gary joined The Lettermen in 1967. Bobby's kids were reaching school age, and his wife wanted him home. I was upset with Bobby's wife for making him choose between her and the group. I was dating Sue at the time and told her, "Don't make me choose between The Lettermen and you because I'll choose The Lettermen. That's my baby. That's my group." Back then, The Lettermen was my self-worth; it was the only thing that gave me confidence. It was hard losing Bobby, but when Gary joined, I loved having my brother with me all the time. At first, people didn't even realize Gary had replaced Bobby—he blended in that well. Of course, it took a little work.

We auditioned quite a few people before Gary joined The Lettermen, but Gary was the only one who could fit in as well as Bobby. When it was Tony, Gary, and I singing, you'd never know it wasn't Tony, Bobby, and me. Early on, people used to think Bobby and I were brothers. Since Gary looked so similar to both of us, we had him dye his hair and eyebrows to look even more like Bobby. Actually, it wasn't until the intermission of Gary's first show that people realized Bobby hadn't been the one onstage singing with Tony and me.

It took us awhile to get Gary onstage. I was ready, and he was ready, but we were both scared to put him out there. For a couple of months, Gary came out with us on the road to watch the shows so he could learn the choreography. Every night, I would have him dress up with all his makeup on, ready to go out there, but Gary was nervous. He had everything down, but we all just kept putting it off. One night though, while we were performing for a college in Ohio, I got a phone call from Bobby saying he couldn't make the show, so we had to use Gary. Gary came out, and we did the first half of our performance. We were getting the same response as usual, and it was a big success. During intermission, when we were backstage in the dressing room, Bobby walked in. He had used a pay phone around the corner to call and say he couldn't make it so we would get Gary onstage. Bobby told us that Gary was going to be fine and we didn't have anything to worry about. We knew that Gary was accepted by the audience. Bobby could go home and be with his wife and children. As we stood backstage listening to the audience holler and scream, Bobby, Gary, and I hugged one another and cried.

Jim Pike, Gary Pike, Tony Butala, Bobby Engemann.
The only time the four famed Lettermen sang onstage together

I have to give it to Bobby. It was a good way to get Gary out onstage for the first time as a Letterman. The only one who knew about Bobby's plan was Sue. She was in the audience at the time and saw Bobby sitting there. Sue was on tour with us because we had started dating more seriously. I told her I wanted to marry her, but before I did, I wanted her to know how hard it was being on tour and what it was like being on the road. It wasn't an easy life. Sue told me she'd go but only if her dad agreed. I called him and explained how I felt about Sue and that I wanted her to understand what life on the road was going to be like if we were to get married. With Bobby as our chaperone, he agreed to let Sue come with us during her two-week vacation as a flight attendant. I underestimated her. While she was out with us, Sue told me, "Well, this is no different than being an airline hostess—sleeping somewhere new every night. I'm already used to this." She always managed to impress me.

CHAPTER 10:
Sue, the Wind Beneath My Wings

A t some point in life, every man has to have his first encounter with the female species; mine happened when I was in kindergarten. My family was living in California at the time, and one day during recess, this cute little curly-haired brunette came up to me and tried to kiss me. Being the sensible boy I was back then, I ran. Well, as you can imagine, that didn't sit too well with the gal, who then proceeded to chase after me. I ran into the boys' room to wait for her, and when she came through the door, I punched her right in the face. Needless to say, I had a lot to learn about women before I met *the one*, but everyone falls in love sooner or later, and for me it happened in May 1967.

Sue Kennedy (Pike)

At the time, Sue was living with her friend Carol in the hills of San Mateo, California, while they both worked as flight attendants for TWA (Trans World Airlines). On a flight to San Francisco, Carol bumped into Ronnie, the drummer for The Lettermen, who was on his way to perform with us for a tour we were doing at the Fairmont Hotel. Carol was sweet and pretty. Ronnie was captivated by her, but when he asked her out, she told him no.

"Why not?"

"Well, I don't know you from Adam."

"How about a double date then? You bring a friend, and I'll bring one of the guys," Ronnie said.

After some hesitation, Carol replied, "All right. When?"

"We have a dark night—that's this following Monday."

I had just gotten to rehearsal Thursday morning when Ronnie came running toward me. He fell on his hands and knees, begging me to go on this date with him. Ronnie said, "I've met this beautiful airline hostess, and she won't go out with me unless it's a double date." I wasn't so sure I wanted to go on a blind date, and I later found out Sue wasn't too thrilled with the idea either, but I thought airline hostesses were pretty cute, so I said, "Okay, it can't be too bad."

Monday night came along, and Ronnie and I were in our hotel rooms getting ready. I pulled out a pair of black mohair pants, a red turtleneck sweater, and a mod herringbone jacket. Ronnie banged on my door at a quarter to six, and we were off. We got to San Mateo just fine, but as soon as we started driving in the hills trying to find the apartment, we got lost. Now this was before everyone carried a cell phone with them. We had no way of calling the girls to tell them we were lost and were going to be late. Meanwhile, both Sue and Carol were just fuming at the idea of being stood up. Sue told Carol if we didn't show by 6:30, she was out of there. Luckily, we finally found the place, but of course, I couldn't find a parking spot. I made Ronnie jump out of the car to get the girls while I double-parked.

Ronnie ran up the stairs to their door. When they answered, he told them, "I'm sorry we're so late; we got lost. Jim can't find a place to park, so he's double-parked. We've got to leave or else we're going to be late for the movie." Ronnie went back down the steps to let me know they were coming, while Sue and Carol locked up the apartment. As they got to the landing, I saw a pretty woman who I suspected was Carol from what Ronnie had told me. She looked at me and then stopped and turned to look behind her. Seconds later, a perky gal stepped onto the landing. She wore a short dress that caused my eyes to go directly to her legs. My first impression was that Sue looked like Twiggy. She had the same haircut and huge green eyes. Sue and Carol came down toward the car, and I apologized to Sue as I opened the car door for her, "I'm so sorry we're late, we got lost."

After we were married, Sue told me why Carol had turned back to her that night: when Carol saw me, she turned to Sue to tell her, "Kennedy, don't ever say I didn't do anything for you."

As soon as Sue stepped onto the landing, she grabbed Carol's arm and whispered, "Carol, that's not one of the musicians, that's one of *them*! I have five of their albums; I love The Lettermen!" Sue had thought she was going on a blind date with one of the musicians since Ronnie was the drummer, but she got me instead.

When Sue got in the car, the first thing she said to me was, "What religion are you?" The question took us both by surprise. I answered "I'm a Mormon." "So am I!" she replied. "I don't know why I asked you that. I haven't been to church since I was a young girl. I've never cared what anyone's religion is." I may not be able to tell you why Sue asked me that question that night, but I'm glad she did. With me being on tour most of the year, and her being a flight attendant, having a relationship took a lot of effort. I don't know if I would have put that much effort into our relationship if we weren't the same religion.

Ronnie and I took our dates to the movies and then out to dinner. While we were at dinner, Sue asked me how old I was. "Thirty," I said. I figured Sue was in her midtwenties, so when I asked for her age, I nearly spilled my milk when she answered, "Twenty-one." But age was never an issue for us. The only time we laugh about it is when we discuss the year a particular song was a hit and I was in college at the time, and Sue was in grammar school.

After our date, as we dropped Sue and Carol off, I leaned over, kissed Sue on the forehead, and said, "Thank you for a really nice evening. I'll be calling you."

We went fishing for our second date. The Lettermen were still playing at the Fairmont, and one Sunday, after our last performance for the night, I drove to San Mateo to pick Sue up and get her to the harbor before three o'clock in the morning. I had chartered a boat for Tony, Bobby, all the musicians, and the two of us. Sue had never been fishing before—had never even held a fishing pole in her hand. I bragged to her about how experienced I was at fishing because growing up in Idaho, I had been fishing practically my whole life. We got on the boat at three, and the captain guided us out into the ocean for a good two hours before he stopped the engine and shouted to everyone, "Okay, there are the poles!" Everyone walked over, grabbed a pole, and found a spot to cast their line. Sue stayed behind to talk to the captain.

"I've never fished before, and I don't know what to do," she told the captain.

He walked over and got a pole for her. "Here's the pole," he said as he pulled the line several times. "I want you to go stand over there, and I'll bait the hook for you." He then showed Sue how to cast her line. Immediately after she did, she caught the first fish. So much for all my bragging. Sue not only caught the first fish, she caught the biggest fish and the most fish that day.

After we were back on shore, I looked in a phone book to find a meat locker to store the fish in. I told them I had some fish and asked if they would clean them, cut them up, and keep them frozen. They said they could. I wanted Sue and her friends to be able to enjoy the fish.

After we dropped the fish off at the meat locker, I turned to Sue and said, "I'm starving. Are you hungry?" By that time, it was four thirty in the afternoon. She didn't really have any food in the house, and we were both so grubby we didn't want to go into a restaurant. I suggested we hit the supermarket by her apartment. "I don't want you cooking," I said as I put two TV dinners in our basket. We got home, I put them in the oven, and after we ate, we lay down on her living room floor and talked for hours. It was the first time for us to really talk, be ourselves, and get to know each other better.

We dated sporadically for several months because of our work schedules. With me singing and Sue flying, we weren't together as much as I would have liked. We talked on the phone every night though, sometimes for as long as three hours. My business manager told me, "Jim, it would be cheaper just to marry the girl than to pay these high phone bills." Long-distance calls were very expensive, but I didn't care. Sue was worth it. Yet, as much as I loved Sue, I was leery of marriage. I had seen my mom and dad's marriage crumble, and I couldn't bear the thought of going through something like that. It wasn't a question of love. I loved Sue more than I thought I could love anyone. I knew no matter how long or hard I looked, I would never find another girl like her, but I was scared of getting married.

It was the first week of August 1968, and at this point, we were both living in Los Angeles. Sue had just come home from a flight, and on our date, she told me, "Jim, it doesn't mean I love you any less, but I'm not going to live waiting for your phone calls anymore. I hardly ever get out when you're away because I sit there and wait for my phone to ring. I get to see you maybe once a month when you're on tour, if I'm lucky enough to fly into a city you're performing in. I'm tired of living for that phone to ring. I can't do it anymore. I have to live my life." I dropped her off after our date, and the next morning, she left for another flight. When she got back, she came over to my place. We were in the dining room when I grabbed onto her shoulders, shook her, and said, "Damn you, damn you, I'm gonna marry you."

"You are?" Her eyes were wide. All I could think was, *I love this woman, and I can't live without her. I guess that means I'm going to have to marry her.*

It was still the beginning of August, and Sue left yet again for another flight. When she got home, I took her to our favorite Chinese restaurant called the Far East Terrace. Before we left for the restaurant, I took some Valium my doctor had prescribed to help relax my throat and voice muscles, but I had taken it on an empty stomach. So we're sitting in the restaurant, I'm drooling, and I can barely hold my fork. I looked at Sue and said, "You know, I think we ought to get married."

Sue didn't say anything at first. She just kept eating. When we got up to leave, Sue looked at me and said, "I'm leaving at ten tomorrow morning for my flight. If you still feel the same way when you wake up, call me." I called her about nine thirty the next day and said, "You know, I think you're right. We should wait." But I was weakening, and she knew it. Sue was only gone a couple of days, but I thought a lot about marriage in those two days. When she came home, I took her back to the Far East Terrace and said to her, "I think we should get married." It makes me laugh now when I think about it, because she was ready. As soon as I said that, she pulled out her flying schedule, and said, "I have the twenty-second, twenty-third, and twenty-fourth off. What day do you want to get married?" We chose the twenty-third, which gave us exactly two and a half weeks to plan a wedding.

When we got back to my house, Sue said to me, "Okay, I'm going to call my mom and tell her. Once I do, you can't take it back." A million things were going through my head, and when I heard her say, "Mom, guess what? I'm getting married," I backed up against the wall and slid down to the floor. I put my hands over my eyes, thinking, *What in the world am I doing?* I loved Sue so much, but I couldn't believe we were getting married.

However, once I got it in my head we were going to be husband and wife, that was it, I was fine. Sue, on the other hand, started panicking. We made a list of everyone we wanted at the wedding. By the time we added family, friends, college friends, and the numerous people I knew in the music industry, we had nearly one thousand people. Finally I pushed the list away from us and said to Sue, "You know, honey, this is a very special time. I don't want it to be like a zoo with all these people. I want it to be special. Let's have it be just you, me, my parents, and your parents. That's it."

August 23, 1968—Mr. and Mrs. Jim Pike

We got married in the Relief Society room in the Studio City ward building. It was the first time Sue's parents had seen each other since their divorce. Her dad was really nervous when he saw Sue's beautiful mother. Gary and Bobby crashed the wedding, which was no surprise to us, but other than the two of them, only our parents were there and, of course, the bishop who married us. At one point, right at the part where the bishop was telling us to bring out the best in each other, Sue said, "Bishop, can you stop?" My whole body froze, and I thought, *Is she going to back out?* Sue was crying, and her nose was running. She looked to her mom and said, "I need a Kleenex." I let out a sigh of relief as her mom got a hanky for her.

We got married on a Friday. On the following Monday, The Lettermen did *The Red Skelton Show* on television and then left for tour. Being on tour was our honeymoon. We've been joined at the hip ever since. I find it funny when a husband retires, and it drives his wife nuts to have him underfoot all the time. Sue and I have been together 24/7 since the day we were wed. Years after we were married, people would come up to us and ask if we were newlyweds because we'd cuddle and hold hands and kiss each other in public. Our love has always been strong. The day I met Sue, I felt that I had known her forever.

Sue and I were meant to be. What are the odds that Ronnie and Carol would be on the same flight? That the one night Ronnie could go out on the date was the night Sue had off? Or that Sue would have asked me what religion I was? I could have asked someone else in the group to go on the date for me, or Sue could have told Carol no, but everything worked out. There were just so many variables that brought us together, I knew it was meant to be; there was no other explanation.

I don't know where I would be without Sue. She's kept me steady these past forty-three years. She's been patient with me. I had quite a temper when we first met, but the first time I lost my temper in front of her, she said, "We're not going to have any of this. You're not your dad, Jim."

"Groupies" is what some people like to call the women who hang all over you after a show. Personally, I refer to them as trouble. When I got married to Sue, I made sure she knew there would be women—lots of women—hanging around us. That was just the way it was. One time, a girl snuck onto our tour bus and took my wardrobe. Come on, my clothes? Another time, Sue and I were coming off the bus when a young woman walked up to me and asked, "Do you swing on your wife?" Before

I had a chance to say no, Sue got between the two of us. With her jaw set, Sue looked the girl right in the eye and said, "No, he does not. You should wash your mouth out with soap."

Another time, we had just finished a concert, and I was making my way backstage toward Sue when this woman came up and said, "Do you remember me, Jim?" She then turned to Sue and said, "I don't know if you know me, but I used to date Jim. I loved him and wanted to marry him. How did you get him?"

Sue and I were both speechless. Finally, Sue was able to say, "Well, I guess he fell in love with me."

The woman just stared at Sue and then back at me before a security officer came over and escorted her out one of the exits. It was rather funny.

No matter where we were, every few months some woman would say, "I used to go out with Jim," or "Do you remember me, Jim?"

Sue had to beat off a few gals here and there. I told her I wasn't interested in any of those women. She just huffed at me and said, "It's that little boy in you that attracts women. You have a sparkle in your eye, and when you smile … you're just so naïve about things!" But my wife knew she didn't have any reason to be jealous. I told her once that she didn't have to come on tour with me, and she said, "Jim, I love you. That's why I married you. But I'm not stupid. I'm not leaving you out on the road while I'm at home alone. You're a good man, but there's no sense throwing you into temptation's fire and seeing if you burn or not. I'm going with you." Now when we're out on the road, I tell Sue, "You don't have much to worry about, sweetie; I'm not fast enough to chase any women."

CHAPTER 11:
There Is Someone Watching Your Footsteps

At Capitol, when the phones would ring, you used to hear, "Capitol Records, home of Nate King Cole," but when they started saying, "Capitol Records, home of The Lettermen," we knew we had made it.

Starting in 1971, The Lettermen spent the entire month of February in Japan. On our first flight to Japan, I thought there must be a politician or someone important to their country on the plane with us because when we landed, there was a red carpet leading to our terminal and hundreds of people waiting. I looked back to see who was on the plane, but as we got off, we heard the crowd shouting, "Rettermen! Rettermen!" because they couldn't pronounce the L. I was overwhelmed.

We soon learned the more the Japanese people respected you, the lower they bowed. Some of these guys would come to meet us and nearly crack their foreheads open on the floor they bowed so low. It was fun and a nice ego boost.

The arenas in Japan held forty thousand people. They were huge. After we performed a song, the audience clapped for us—seven claps, one after the other: *clap—clap—clap—clap—clap—clap—clap*. We thought we were sinking. Turns out, they don't applaud like an American audience; getting seven claps was like getting a standing ovation. Usually artists will get between four and five. The audiences in Japan loved us. In *Billboard* magazine, we were number one in Japan, even over The Beach Boys and The Beatles.

I loved the people there. They were so respectful. When we'd wake up in the morning and open our hotel room door, there would be flowers, origami, stuffed animals, and silk scarves all around the door. We would have to buy suitcase after suitcase to take all those gifts home. We never heard anyone leave these gifts. They just came and went quietly. It was very considerate of them.

The Lettermen Live in Japan

One of the strangest and most remarkable things I noticed about Japan was that there were tons of bicycles everywhere and not a single padlock. There was an honor among the people, and I appreciated that. The Japanese were always on time. If the limo driver told us he'd be in the lobby at ten, he was there at exactly ten. Their word meant everything to them.

There was always a very strict security team around us in Japan. I don't think Sue ever had to hold her own purse. At that time, Sue had long blonde hair, and I always thought it was funny that people would come up and touch it. I also found it amusing to listen to the announcements they'd do over the big loudspeakers downtown. It would be a bunch of Japanese words and then "McDonald's!" or "Coca-Cola!" I got the biggest kick out of that.

"Sealed with a Kiss" was our largest record over there and was released as a single. Then I recorded "Love," and that song blew every other song out of proportion in Japan. One of the coolest things that ever happened to me while I was in The Lettermen was when NASA decided to place a recording of "American Popular Music" called the *United Nations Album* in the time capsule on the moon, and one of the songs they chose was my solo "Love."

I recorded the song "Love" after our first visit to Japan. When we went back in '72, the song was number one in Japan. I sang it in English first because the audience wanted to hear it just the way it was on the radio. Then the announcer got up and told the audience I was going to sing the song in Japanese. The place went nuts, especially for a Japanese audience. I came out on stage with the song written in their language on a piece of paper because I didn't know it by heart yet. I wanted to sing it correctly, so a woman from Capitol Records taught me the song phonetically. I can't speak Japanese, but I could sing that song perfectly the way she taught me. I had the paper but couldn't read it because they shut off all the lights except for one shining on my face. I turned my back to the light and held up the paper so I could read it. Everyone was laughing so hard, it was unbelievable. What a memory!

The Japanese people were so sweet. When we left the first time and were going through customs, we turned to see many fans with their noses and hands pressed up against the glass, watching us and crying. We were crying too! We put our own hands up against the glass. They were such a loving people. They loved the softer harmonies. And I think they liked the idea that our image was very clean and we were "all-American."

CHAPTER 12:
Silly Boy

Gary Pike, Jim Pike, Tony Butala

During the months The Lettermen recorded, we were at the big Capitol tower every day. After work, Tony, Bobby, and I would walk out to the parking lot where a group of boys waited for us to get out so they could sing with us. It was fun. The three of us and the five of them would stand in that parking lot, sometimes for over an hour, just singing. When they got older, those boys became The Beach Boys, and we'd still get together sometimes and sing. One day, I told Brian Wilson,

"You oughta write The Lettermen a surfing ballad." I waited and waited to hear from him. Then one day I heard, *"Little surfer, little one ..."* on the radio and thought, *Oh no, it was too good. They kept it.* It was a good song. I figured the other guys told Brian, "No way are we giving that song up."

After that, the next summer I decided The Lettermen really needed a summer theme song—something everyone would want playing on the radio during their summer. I called Hollywood Sheet Music and asked, "Are there any lyrics to 'Theme from a Summer Place'?" They told me they had just come in. I asked them to hold a copy for me, and I'd be right over. That song had a four-part harmony to it, so I sang the high and second part. I hoped this song would be a hit for us because we hadn't had one in a while, but rather than staying in town to find out, I decided to go fishing in Idaho to clear my head. I went to Williams Lake, which was in an area you could get to only by mule or horseback. I liked being up there by myself; I wasn't even thinking about "Theme from a Summer Place." After a few days alone, I heard this clopping sound and turned around. One of the forest rangers on a mule was holding a note above his head and waving at me. "Got a note from California for you, Jim!" he hollered. The note was from my manager, Jess Rand. It read: "Get back to Hollywood; we've got a smash hit with 'Theme from a Summer Place.'" I was so excited; I packed up all my gear right then and there and headed home.

The Lettermen were in *Billboard* magazine all the time. They wrote articles about us, and we had our picture on the front cover several times in the sixties because we'd have three or four albums on *Billboard*'s Top 200 National Best-Selling Albums at the same time. Since we were making so many albums, they'd all hit the charts at the same time. However, you're only as good as your last hit, and when you become unpopular, there's not a whole lot you can do about it.

During the early seventies, sometime after Gary had joined The Lettermen, we were asked to be on *The Mike Douglas Show,* an hour-long daytime variety television show stationed out of Philadelphia. We had done several of Mike's shows before and had reached the point where we could be his guest celebrity stars. William Morris Agency called us and offered the position of being Mike's cohosts for an entire week. We were each given permission to invite one person to be on the show at some point during the week. Tony, who had grown up with Connie Stevens, asked her to come on. She used to sing four-part harmonies with Tony,

Jim Blaine, and another guy—the same kind of harmonies The Damons used to sing. When Connie came on, Gary, Tony, and I sang "Blue World" with her. I invited Sue Raney, a great jazz singer who used to sing on the same show with The Four Freshmen, to come on. She had amazing talent and sang a beautiful solo.

The Lettermen had a lot of memorable moments and many laughable ones. There was one time onstage, I think we were playing at the University of Texas, and some kids in the front row started snickering and laughing. We were wearing black pants, red Ivy League shirts, and gray sweaters. We looked around us, trying to figure out what was so funny. I suddenly looked down and saw the red corner of my shirt sticking out through the fly in my pants. Then the whole audience looked to see what I was looking at, and the place went nuts. I just turned around, tucked in my shirt, zipped up my fly, took a bow, and kept on singing.

Little things like that happened all the time. Once I had a really bad cold, and there was a part in our act where we did impressions of other vocal groups. Then, in between, we would explain to the audience how these guys happened onto their hits accidently, like the one guy who took Alka Seltzer, went to the record studio, and—bam! His nasal passages cleared up, and he sounded amazing! For this one particular scene, I was playing James Cagney, and Tony was doing the Professor. I was saying, "You dirty rat … ," and at the end, I was supposed to laugh through my nose. Well, I started to laugh, and a huge snot bubble came out of my nose! There it was in the spotlight, glistening, and then it went *boom* all over my sweater. I think that's the first time I ever got a red face as an adult in front of an audience.

One of my most embarrassing performances happened at the Crescendo in Hollywood. I walked out onstage, and there was my dad, sitting at a table with Paul Newman and Joanne Woodward. My dad was showing Paul his tie, which looked like it had a rope twisted around it, but if you turned it to the side, it said, "Bull Shit." I nearly threw up at the idea that these celebrities would find out this yo-yo cowboy was my dad. I just kept singing, and every once in a while, I'd glance over at my dad. I think I was so embarrassed because I was entering a new social status. Back then, I was ashamed of where I had come from and who my parents were.

At the time, the Waldorf Astoria was the biggest and most distinguished supper club in the United States. The Empire Room was where all the big entertainers, such as Ella Fitzgerald and Tony Bennett, performed, and the William Morris Agency always booked us there during prom season. The stage in the Empire Room was put together in three different pieces. I was in the middle of the stage singing "Impossible Dream," which was popular at the time because it was still being sung on Broadway. Suddenly the two pieces I was standing over split. I went down about three feet, ripping my tux and skinning my knee in the process. It must have been pretty funny to see my face in the spotlight one moment and then gone the next. Everyone was laughing. It was especially embarrassing because I knew Roddy McDowall and Patrick Wayne were in the audience. A crew of men ran over to pull me up. They moved the stage back together, but when we went to the next song, I made sure I was standing over a solid platform piece.

I remember a time when all three of us got food poisoning. We were playing in a big arena that held about forty thousand students at the University of Oklahoma. We had eaten some hot dogs at a concession stand before the show. We ended up so sick that one of us would sing a solo while the other two ran offstage to throw up and then return. We took turns singing and running offstage. It was like playing hot potato. I was humiliated, but the audience was screaming and laughing. It was so funny to them, and they loved it because they were getting a different show from what we normally did. This one was mostly solos.

When Bobby and I started singing together, I was still young, having left my family at the age of seventeen. Bobby's parents welcomed me in, and I became really close to his family. At times, it felt as if Bobby and I were brothers. While living in California, we entered a quartet contest. About a week before the competition, Bobby and I found these two girls who could sing. We taught them their parts to "Lullaby of Broadway" with really modern harmonies and rehearsed a couple of times. We ended up winning. I felt sorry for the other groups. They had been practicing for months, while we just threw a group together at the last minute and won. I suppose it just goes to show you how well Bobby and I could sing together.

Bobby and I also double-dated a lot. When we were younger, we wouldn't date girls unless they could sing. We would teach them songs of The Four Freshmen or The Damons so we could sit in the car and sing these four-part harmonies. We got over that eventually, and obviously if we liked someone who couldn't sing, it wasn't a deal breaker. I mean, when I first met Sue, she told me right off the bat she didn't sing and especially wouldn't in front of me. That didn't stop me from falling in love with her. There was one time though, Bobby and I went out on a double date, and he ended up dating the mother of the gal I was dating! Bobby liked older women, whereas I liked them younger. I got a call from Bobby's mother a couple of days later. She said, "I understand you went on a double date with Bobby, and he went out with the mother, and you went out with the daughter."

"That's right."

"I'm worried about my son."

"I'm worried about him too!"

For a while after that, everybody would tease us and say, "Oh yeah, Jim and Bobby go out on dates. Bobby goes with the mothers, and Jim takes out the daughters!"

In 1961, we went out on our first tours in a station wagon. Then we got a Dodge motor home. Our brand-new Dodge motor home looked like the Bat Mobile. They were really aerodynamic back in the early sixties. We were traveling in the Appalachian Mountains of Tennessee when we pulled up to this little service station with a single gas pump with a glass ball on top where you could see the gas. To check the engine, you had to come in through the door like you were entering and pick up the hood to expose the Dodge motor. The service man came onto the bus in his blue overalls, with a red handkerchief in one hand, saying, "Hi, y'all. Boy, this sure is a fancy rig." He looked up and gasped, "Tay-Vay?" and nearly fell back out of the vehicle. We had a big television mounted to the wall of the motor home; he had never seen one in a motor home before.

Eventually, The Lettermen got a Greyhound bus we had converted so we could travel with all our clothes hanging up. That way, we didn't have to iron them every night. We also had plenty of space for our road manager and the musicians to sleep. Besides our bus, we had a converted mail truck that stored all of our sound equipment, generators, PA systems, and lighting. Basically, we were self-contained. We could have put on an entire show in the middle of the desert if we had wanted to. One time though, while in the middle of Indiana, we weren't with the bus, but the musicians and everyone else were together. When they finally showed up at rehearsal the following afternoon, they said, "You won't believe what happened at three o'clock this morning." They had pulled off the side of the road to get some sleep. It was so foggy they couldn't really see where they were. Then someone started banging on their doors. When they opened the doors, there was a farmer with a sheriff who wanted to search the bus. There had been some cattle rustling in that area. Imagine that. In this day and age, there was still cattle rustling going on, and because of it, our guys got searched in an Indiana cow pasture.

Once, when we were in Fresno to do our opening night show with George Burns, I took Tony fishing. I had just purchased a brand-new gun-metal gray Pontiac Grand Prix with red leather upholstery. It was the first car I had ever owned that was brand-new. We took it up to a lake with all our gear in the back. We got our stuff out of the car, and Tony was on the dock, literally with one foot on the dock and one ready to step into the boat. I pulled the keys out of the car, locked the door, and bent down to pick up my fishing pole when the car started rolling. I couldn't get my keys out of my pocket, so I got in front of the car to try to stop it, but it kept going. My feet were slipping out from under me, so I pushed hard against the hood and then threw myself to the left of the car. No sooner had I leaped out of the way than the car went off the edge of the road and dove straight into the water. My first new car was at the bottom of a lake. Meanwhile, Tony just stared, mouth wide open, one foot still hovering in the air. We called AAA, and they had to bring a special crane to pull it out. After it was on shore, I opened the driver's door, and water came pouring out of it. Being the fisherman I was, I hoped there would at least be one trout in there, but no such luck. I finally got my key out of my pocket, put it in the ignition, and willed my car to start. But no chance; my first new car was dead.

There were times we missed shows. We came into a city once, pulled up to the arena, and asked where we were supposed to go. The student, seeing "The Lettermen" on the bus, looked at us confused and then said, "The concert was this afternoon." It had been scheduled at one in the afternoon, but we had shown up at three. We thought it was an evening concert since that was what our schedule read. We had to reschedule another concert with the school and return everyone's money.

Another time, we were in Chicago and thought the show was the next day. Sue and I turned our car in to get serviced and walked to a movie theater. When we got back to our hotel around eleven o'clock that night, the message light was blinking on our phone. "Sue, Jim, the concert is tonight." The show was already over by the time we got the message. There had been a typo mistake on the schedule. We had a reputation for always showing up for our shows, so it was frustrating whenever we missed one, even if it was due to a schedule error.

It was tradition that during the last show of every tour, whether we were going home for Christmas or the summer, the crew would play jokes on one another. When we were doing college shows, our road manager would go out into the crowd during the first half and find the homecoming queen or some other pretty girl. She would come onstage to give me a note that would have specific jokes or some comedy on it about the girl delivering the note. It was just part of our act. Well, one time, the guys dressed up one of our road crew members to look like a woman. Sharon, Gary's wife, was quite tall, and her pantyhose and shoes fit him. Then Sue gave him her fur coat to wear. He came up at the beginning of the second half of the show as the "note girl." I couldn't manage to joke or flirt with him as he handed me a Polaroid folded up in an envelope. When I opened it, it was a picture of all the musicians and crew standing in a row naked. I was speechless for a few moments. I didn't know what to say. I quickly moved onto the next part of our show, but I've always wondered who took that picture.

Another time at one of these shows, the homecoming queen was well endowed. I didn't mean to make a joke, but it stunned me so much I went, "Holy cow!" right over the microphone. The audience laughed for fifteen minutes straight. It was spontaneous. I didn't mean to say it, but it turned out to be really funny to the kids.

When you're on stage, every second counts. A minute of dead space feels like an hour. Once, our road manager found the homecoming queen and gave her the note, but she gave it to another girl to take up to us. I think she was just trying to be a good friend. Well, we're standing up onstage, and on the other side, a young woman with braces on her legs was walking toward us very slowly. We could hear the *clink-clink* of her braces as the clock ticked by. It would have taken her a couple of minutes to get to us, so without thinking, I ran up to her. I took the note, picked her up, and turned her around so she could walk the other way. The audience was screaming. They probably thought it was part of the act, but I felt bad. I never wanted to hurt anyone's feelings. I didn't do it for a laugh, but I was afraid of dead silence. We ended up going straight into a song. How could I have made a joke about her?

At one school, the basketball coach made the students create a space for us to perform, or else he wouldn't let them have the concert. The floor was made rather roughly out of thick, dusty plywood. When it was time, the homecoming queen came up to me, handed me the note, smiled, and waved to the crowd. She started walking away, but her toe caught the edge of the plywood. It happened as if in slow motion: the spotlight was shining on her face, she was catapulted up, and then she fell down, dust flying up in the air as she hit the floor. She managed to keep her poise and demeanor the entire time though. There was dead silence until Bobby started laughing, and then I started. Next thing I knew, the whole audience was laughing. I give credit to the girl though. She stood up, still smiling and waving as any homecoming queen would do, and walked back to the crowd. Again though, I didn't have any jokes to tell. The comedy worked out well most of the time, but every once in a while, when something like that happened, we just had to wing it.

Around 1971, The Lettermen were playing at the Georgia Institute of Technology in Atlanta. While I was walking around outside with Sue and Gary, my knee locked up, and there was pain like crazy. They rushed me to the emergency room. I hadn't gone to a doctor about my knee since I was medically discharged from the navy. When the doctors in the emergency room took a look at my knee, they told me I had to find a specialist and get an operation when we returned home, which I did. In the meantime, the doctors wrapped a soft cast around my knee and gave me a shot for the pain. We were playing that night, so I had to slit my tux pants to accommodate the cast. I ended up going out onstage with a cane in one hand and a microphone in the other. The college kids seemed to get a big hoot out of me performing onstage holding a cane with a cast on my leg.

Before returning home to have that second surgery, we played at the Palmer House in Chicago. After one particular show, June Lockhart, a very beautiful and well-known actress, came up to us backstage and introduced herself. I could tell she had her eyes on me, but Sue was with me. We said hello to one another, and Sue and I went to our room. About an hour later, June Lockhart actually came to our room. She was a nice person and a good actress, but still, her flirting made both Sue and me uncomfortable.

A couple of days later, I had my second surgery. While I was lying in the hospital room, my bed curtain parted, and in came June Lockhart holding flowers! Sue arrived at the hospital about ten minutes after June did. As Sue walked toward the orthopedic room, kids were coming out on their crutches saying, "Lassie's mom is here."

Sue came into my room and said, "Hi, honey. Hi, June."

I turned to Sue and said, "Hi, honey, I'm so glad to see you."

June was there for about five more minutes and then left. It was a thrill to have someone that famous come to the hospital to see me. I didn't mind having a nice boost to my ego every once in a while.

My third and final knee surgery happened a day before we performed at the Fairmont in San Francisco. The surgery was only supposed to be a thirty-minute procedure, but I was in there for five hours. A couple of pieces of cartilage were sliding around and sticking to the sides and back of my knee, so it was hard for the doctors to get them out. When they were done operating on me that evening, I went home. The next morning, I got on a plane to San Francisco, and that night we were doing a show. I had a cast on again, so I had to split my tux pants once more. I had a temperature of over 103 degrees Fahrenheit, and I was onstage that night just sweating. The newspapers the next day said something like, "The show must go on. Jim Pike performs even though he had a fever and a cast on his leg."

Karl Engemann, Jim Pike, Gary Pike, Stanley Gortikov,
Jess Rand, Tony Butala, Kelly Gordon

CHAPTER 13:
Don't Know What I'm Going Through

My first voice problem happened in 1969, and I took about six months off from singing. I got Doug Curran to take my place. I had sung with Doug at BYU, and I knew Tony would like him because he had a nice solo voice. Doug was a very big and tall man with a size thirteen shoe. We had a heck of a time getting his wardrobe together. He was kind though, and he actually met his wife while on the road taking my place.

Even though I wasn't singing, I was doing everything else: I would go out to practices and make sure the act was good. I'd tell the guys what to say, how to stand, and how to move. I did everything so our group could go out there and continue making money. Then The Lettermen had the summer off that year, and people were calling and saying, "We miss Jim Pike."

The first time I lost my voice was the scariest. Nothing like that had ever happened to me. I panicked and went to see a world-famous vocal coach. Gene Byrum was very well known in the industry and had worked with numerous actors and singers. The first time I met him was January '69. I was nervous meeting him because he was so famous. We tried some vocal exercises, but nothing happened because my voice was closed off. He took a liking to me, and we became really close. For some reason, he chose me to be the son he never had. I was his favorite pupil, which helped me relax when I was around him. I knew he liked me as a person. Gene had this big voice. He had been an amazing opera singer in his day. When I would come into the studio, the room would rumble with his voice as he'd say, "Hello there, Jim."

Gene was the greatest. He was a genius. Any actor or singer who had voice problems that needed to be fixed fast went to see Gene. He had worked with Judy Garland, Frank Sinatra, and Tony Bennett. He once worked with a woman from England whose vocal cord had been accidentally cut by a doctor. Gene worked with her until she was able to sing again.

I brought a microphone, a little speaker, and the background tapes of our shows. I sang into the microphone so Gene could hear me well enough over the background of every song. But I just didn't make any progress with him. I couldn't even voice, *"ahahahahah."* I felt like my life was over. I couldn't do my voice exercises either. Gene was great, but something inside of me was paralyzing my diaphragm and wouldn't let Gene help me.

I was telling this to Bob Flanigan of The Four Freshmen one day when he said to me, "You know, Jim, when I lost my voice, they sent me to see a psychiatrist."

"A shrink? My problem is my voice not my head."

"I'm telling you, I saw Dr. Kranzdorf—Charles Kranzdorf—and it made a huge difference."

"I don't know. I don't feel that would really help me."

"Look, just let me give you his number. It's yours to do with what you want."

I carried Dr. Kranzdorf's number with me for about a week before I decided to give him a call. When I told Gene I was going to meet with the doctor, he said he didn't believe in psychiatry. "Jim, you're not kooky in the head. What do you need psychiatry for?" Gene told me if I went to see Kranzdorf that he wouldn't work with me anymore. I decided I just wouldn't tell him. It was hard for me to do, as I'm an honest person, but I was desperate.

Dr. Charles Kranzdorf or, as he later became to me, Charlie, was a group singer and knew what I was going through. We bonded, and that helped me feel at ease with him. *Cool* wasn't exactly the word I thought I would ever use to describe a psychiatrist, but when I think of Charlie, there's no other word for him—he was cool. The very first day we met, he wanted to do hypnosis on me, but I knew that I couldn't be hypnotized.

"I want you to arm wrestle with me, Jim." I was stronger than Charlie, and he couldn't put my arm down. We tussled for a bit before I beat him. Then Charlie said, "Now let me try the hypnosis."

I never fell asleep; I just relaxed back into the chair I was sitting in and listened to his soothing voice. "Jim, the next time we arm wrestle, you are not going to resist. This time I am going to be able to beat you."

I didn't think I was hypnotized, but I couldn't believe how weak I was when we arm wrestled again. I was struggling to fight back, but Charlie simply put my arm down and said, "So you don't think you can be hypnotized, huh? I rest my case." I stared at him, stunned.

I was amazed the hypnosis had worked so well, but Charlie warned me, "We've got to find out why you're so sad. It'll take awhile. Right now the hypnosis will work, but it's just a Band-Aid to get you back in the group and save your career."

Warning given, Charlie made me a hypnosis tape. The tape said, "Every time you sing, you're going to sing effortlessly, with ease, with no strain in your voice, and you will make progress with your vocal coach."

I listened to that tape before each time I tried to sing. After the first day of listening to it, I went back to Gene. I didn't dare say a word to him about the hypnosis, but I immediately started making progress and started singing the way I used to. I finally got to the point where I could do the whole show over the microphone without straining my voice anywhere. It was amazing. Best of all, I was finally allowing myself to let loose. Doug left, and I got back in with the group after a six-month leave. My voice and I were good for almost five years.

CHAPTER 14:
Hold Your Head Up High

 "THE LETTERMEN"
NATIONAL FAN CLUB
140 S. BEVERLY DRIVE
BEVERLY HILLS, CALIF.

Tony Butala, Jim Pike, Gary Pike

I'll never forget the first night I came back after working with Charlie and Gene. The Lettermen were scheduled to perform at the Fairmont Hotel. Two days before the show, I got a phone call. Charlie was dead. He was jogging in front of his house, had a heart attack, and collapsed. At that time, Charlie and I were still working together, and I was still leaning on him. In fact, he was coming to San Francisco to see my first show back with the group. Charlie's death was devastating, but Tony and Gary were counting on me. Doug was backstage dressed and ready to go on in case anything should go wrong, but I didn't need him to step in.

That first night, after we finished singing, my brother Gary and I ran off the stage and collapsed in each other's arms. We were both so happy; we were crying because I had managed to do the whole show.

During the show, though, when I was singing "Impossible Dream," my voice cracked. I couldn't believe it. I was so upset that when it was time for me to hit the last note of that song, I went for it. Gene had told me not to go too high, but I had to prove myself. I had to prove I was stronger than my voice. I hit the high note and held it as long as I could. The place went nuts—it was terrific—but I realized the mistake I had just made. The second I thought I had to prove "I'm stronger than my voice" was the moment I was no longer one with my voice. We were fighting against each other, and what a fight it turned out to be.

When Sue and I got back to our hotel room, she called Gene's room to see what he thought of the show. Betty, his wife, answered and said she and Gene were packing.

"You're packing!" I could hear the anger in Sue's voice from across the room.

"We're going to Las Vegas to see another singer who's having problems."

"You can't leave! It's costing Jim thousands of dollars to have you stay here for this event. How can you walk out on him? He needs you for support."

"Gene says Jim shouldn't have hit that high note. If Jim isn't going to listen to him, Gene has other singers he can be helping."

"Well, doesn't Gene, who considers Jim his son, understand why he hit that note? He won't hit that note again for the rest of the time we're here. He had to hit it tonight to redeem himself." By this time, Sue was standing to her full height with one hand on her hip. "You tell Gene, if he doesn't understand Jim like he claims he does, then he can just go ahead, pack his bags, and go to Las Vegas because we don't want him here." Sue slammed the phone back on the receiver.

A minute later, Gene called back and apologized. He said he finally understood why I needed to hit that note, and he would stay. I lost Gene within a couple of years though. He died of cancer. We were in Florida doing a concert when we got the phone call. I cried and cried. I loved Gene. He still coached me even after he was diagnosed with cancer. He closed up his studio and stayed in his home. It was so bad he spent most of his days lying on the couch. He canceled everyone's appointments but mine. I was the only person he'd work with. I remember when I'd go into Gene's home, I would get a whiff of the nauseating smell from the chemotherapy. He was there though, and I worked with him. I couldn't believe I was never going to see him again.

"My Way" was a big hit by Sinatra when we were headlining in Las Vegas at the Flamingo's main room. I learned the lyrics and started singing it in the show. It was loud and strong, and I would get huge, roaring, standing ovations. The Las Vegas newspapers were printing things like, "If you want to hear 'My Way' done better than Frank Sinatra, you need to go hear Jim Pike and The Lettermen." It was an amazing feeling. I was singing the best I had sung in years.

Suddenly, I started to have voice problems again. I figured I was probably trying too hard because when I pushed the big notes, people would come out of their seats and roar. Why did I have to have so much approval? I also sang the high and full voice parts because I was the only one who could do them and make them last. But singing with a big voice was the one thing Gene hadn't taught me how to do properly. He had always taught me these head tones so I wouldn't strain my voice. Gene passed away before we could work with big tones. It was also hard to sing in a room full of smoke. All of us slept with huge humidifiers spraying in our faces to keep our voices strong. I also felt I had to live up to the claims that my singing of "My Way" was better than Frank Sinatra's. I put a lot of pressure on myself. Doctors told me if I continued to go out on long tours and belt every song, I was going to end up ruining my voice. Even though this scared me, I had to sing. Singing was my worth, my life, and my reason for living.

I kept getting worse and worse. While on a tour in Washington, DC, my voice got really bad. I broke down and went to see a doctor, who said, "Your vocal cords are bleeding. I don't want you to sing anymore." The club we were playing in decided to sue us because of it. Imagine that. I'm the one who loses my voice, and they're the ones who want to sue. We were losing money, and I felt horrible about it. We had to cut our tour short and go home. I went on voice rest for nearly two months.

It was a vicious cycle that quickly spun out of control. My voice would get bad, and I would see a doctor. I would be put on voice rest, and my voice would get better for a while. Then my voice would get bad, and I would see a doctor … you get the picture. It reached a breaking point in 1973. We finished our tour with the Holiday House in Monroeville,

Pennsylvania, and then we were off for the holidays. I didn't want to hold the group back any longer. During the entire holiday season, I agonized over what to do. Finally, I had to admit I couldn't continue to do tours. I made the decision to replace myself—again. This time, I got my brother Donny.

Donny Pike, who was actually born Donny Unangst, was thirteen years younger than me. Donny's father died when he was three, and in a way, I became his caretaker, just like I watched over and cared for Gary. When I asked Donny to join us, we agreed to change his last name to Pike. That way, The Lettermen would still have two Pike brothers in it.

When Donny first replaced me, I was still able to sing on records. Being onstage and belting over the smoke and orchestra every night tired my voice and caused my vocal cords to bleed. When I had time to rest my voice, I could sing one or two songs in the studio, so the records we sold still had my voice on them along with Tony and Gary's. We were still having hits.

When my voice started to go bad again in Vegas, I worked with a couple of different vocal coaches since the two men, Gene and Charlie, who had done so much for me, were gone. The coaches and lessons didn't do anything though. I went back to see a doctor and was taken aback when he told me my vocal cords weren't bleeding this time.

I pulled at my hair. "Darn it! Listen to me! I know they're bleeding. I can feel it!"

The doctor shook his head. "Jim, I'm looking right at them. They're perfectly fine."

"But I—can—feel—it."

"Then you're feeling something else because your vocal cords aren't bleeding. I suggest you see another kind of doctor."

As much as I hated to admit it, I had to accept that my voice wasn't the problem. It was time to find another psychiatrist.

CHAPTER 15:
Like Needles and Pins

I was still attending social functions when I lost my voice for the second time. People would come up to me and want to talk, but it seemed the more I signaled I couldn't speak, the more questions they would ask me. People want to know what you sound like when your voice leaves you. I could barely manage a strained whisper, and that was if I put my mouth right next to someone's ear. Sue had to speak for me, which was embarrassing and frustrating. I finally got to the point that, when people approached me, I would just walk away. Eventually I stopped putting myself in those situations, only associating with a few close friends and family. I became a hermit in my own home for about a year before I ended up at Edgemont. It was a horrible time in my life. I couldn't verbalize my frustration, so I turned my anger inward, and my depression got worse and worse.

After Charlie died, I tried to find another psychiatrist, especially since the hypnosis tape stopped working. None of the psychiatrists worked out. I now understood the reason Gene had been so against me seeing a psychiatrist in the first place. Most of them seemed crazier than I was. One actually talked to me in the third person. They didn't have what Charlie had, so I walked out on doctor after doctor.

Charlie's wife was the one who introduced me to Dr. Sheldon Kardiner. I liked him. If I said, "I'll commit suicide," Dr. Kardiner would say, "Go ahead. It's all up to you." He was real, and he made sure I knew that I had to do the work—he wasn't going to do it for me, and I couldn't rely on him for a cure. He reminded me of Charlie when he told me I would be the one to tell him when I didn't need to see him anymore.

I had all the confidence in the world when I was with Dr. Kardiner. He'd say, "Jim, just so you know, if you were a ditch digger, your back would have gone out." He was trying to get me to see that my symptoms of depression were all coming from me. It didn't matter what I did or what my profession was, I was stuck in this situation until I fixed my problems.

After two years of seeing Dr. Kardiner and still having voice problems, he suggested I go to UCLA and take a battery of tests. I went over there and spent about two days testing. Afterward, I went back to his office, where he said to me, "Jim, I don't know how to tell you this, but you have a tremendous rage inside of you that you're refusing to deal with to avoid becoming like your father since he was such an angry person. I know you don't want to be angry, but you are. There's so much anger inside of you that you're willing to shut yourself off so you won't hurt others or want to commit suicide. You've been lying to me and to yourself for two years by running around this hot spot. Now we're going to make some progress. I'm going to put you on medication to lower your defenses."

He put me on a semitranquilizer. I thought it was going to make me feel better, but after a week of taking the medicine, I experienced a severe depression. The tranquilizer lowered my defenses, so all the garbage I'd been hiding for years came out, but the depression was a horrible side affect. Suicide suddenly became a serious issue for me. Every morning when I woke up, I would think, *Is this the day I'm actually gonna do it?*

Depression is an ugly thing, and mine was a deep, dark, nasty one. When I confided in Dr. Kardiner how I was feeling, he said, "Jim, we have to deal with this. You're so scared; you really think you're going to do something." So on top of the tranquilizers, he started giving me antidepressants. It didn't work though.

It finally came to a breaking point. I wasn't feeling well that entire day. I was more depressed than I had been in a while. Sue took me to see Dr. Kardiner around eleven o'clock in the morning. He gave me a tranquilizer that was supposed to knock out a horse, but it didn't do a thing.

At seven o'clock in the evening, at our home in Toluca Lake, California, I was lying on the floor, twisting and screaming from the pain. Sue was shaking and crying so hard. She tried to hold me down when my body started to bounce around on the floor. I couldn't feel anything but cold. It was as if an icy hand was squeezing my heart and lungs. My body was fighting so hard against that hand, I was out of control. The worst part was that my mind was clear. I could hear and see everything going on, but I couldn't control my body. It was as if my mind and body had separated, and I was forced to stand aside and watch myself twist up in horror and anguish. At one point, I saw Sue on the phone and heard her speaking to Dr. Kardiner. Her shoulders were hunched over, and she shook as tears ran down her face, but I couldn't get to her. I couldn't tell her everything would be all right—I didn't believe everything would be all right.

Sue managed to get me into the car and drive me to Dr. Kardiner's office. He gave me a second shot that should have definitely knocked me out, but by the time we got back home, the pain was more intense, and my body was more out of control. Sue called Dr. Kardiner again. Dr. Kardiner told Sue to hide all our guns and knives and not to leave my side while he arranged for my admittance to a hospital. At nine o'clock that night, Sue drove me to the mental hospital in Hollywood. I was relieved and knew I would be safe there.

I spent a week sitting in a small, white room with Sue by my side. The only light came from a single bulb in the ceiling and from the little television Sue brought me. Sometimes Sue would talk to me, but for the most part, she just sat there while I worked on the crossword puzzles she gave me, or she'd lay in bed next to me while I stared at the ceiling. I didn't know what to say or do. I felt like I wasn't myself.

It turns out admitting myself to the hospital was one of the best things I ever did. Every morning, I felt better. When I felt I was okay to leave the room, I started going to group therapy at the hospital. There were all kinds of guys in there, and we talked about everything.

I later found out that what I had experienced that horrible night was what doctors call a "peak out." It is like a boil being broken. Dr. Kardiner said, "You got all the way down to the bottom. You got all the bad stuff out." Dr. Kardiner took me off the tranquilizers and put me only on antidepressants, and I was released from the hospital. I'm a much happier man today than I ever was back then.

CHAPTER 16:
Take My Hand, Take My Whole Life Too

From day one, Tony had wanted The Lettermen to be his group. So in late 1975, he made his move. There was a clause in The Lettermen contract that said if one of us couldn't perform for a certain amount of time, the other partner had the right to buy that person out. And that's just what Tony did.

After Bobby left in 1967, Tony and I became 50/50 partners; that way neither of us had complete control. Bobby had wanted to sell me his third so I would own two-thirds of The Lettermen, but it was illegal for him to do that. Instead, I got half, and Tony got half. Even though I owned half of The Lettermen, there was still that clause, which Tony used to his advantage. He did have a right to buy me out, but he could have chosen not to. Unfortunately, that wasn't the choice Tony made.

Soon after getting out of the hospital in December '75, Sue and I flew back to Pennsylvania to meet up with Tony. Obviously, I had other things on my mind, but I still managed to put together an agenda for The Lettermen for the first part of 1976. I had also taken the time to do research and create a list of the tunes to be recorded, along with the arrangements. When we got to the Holiday House, I saw Tony standing there. He came up, gave me a huge hug, and told me everything was going to be okay. I gave him the stack of paperwork I had brought, and then Sue and I were off to catch the next plane home.

The very next morning—at seven o'clock in the morning!—the doorbell rang. An attorney stood in my doorway and served me the papers that said if I couldn't perform before an arbitration board, Tony would get the group. I felt like I had been punched in the stomach. Tony had looked straight at me, with tears in his eyes, and told me everything would work out. Well, I guess he meant everything would work out for him.

Tony had always wanted to be the leader of the group, and here was his opportunity. In January 1976, just days after he told me everything would be all right, Tony used that contract clause as his weapon. He forced me out of the group because I couldn't sing. And he was right; I couldn't sing. I wasn't sure I would ever be able to sing again.

I hired an attorney. I believed The Lettermen name was worth at least three million dollars. I should have gotten half of that. Instead, I settled for much less. I was scared because I had no voice, a wife, and a home to take care of, and there was no fight left in me.

Donny and Gary stayed in The Lettermen even after I sold the name, but it didn't take long for Tony to get them out of the group too. Tony let them go when their contracts came up. I think it's because he didn't want any Pikes singing with the group.

Once, when we were traveling between shows, Sue and I pulled up to a gas station and went in to pay for the gas. The Lettermen bus with the musicians drove in right behind us.

"Hey," I said to the cashier, "twenty dollars on pump number three."

"I know you! Aren't you in that band ... The Lettermen, right?"

"Yeah, I am." I handed him my Lettermen credit card.

"Yeah, we just had the blonde guy, Jim Pike in here. I know because he signed his name. Maybe two hours ago. Nice guy." The cashier swiped my card and handed it back to me.

"Thanks." I didn't bother to correct the man, but when I looked over at Sue and a couple of the musicians, I knew they were thinking the same thing: *Tony.*

After I left, The Lettermen never had another hit or a charted album. When their contract was up with Capitol Records, they didn't get a renewal. Dave Cavanaugh, a famous producer at Capitol who had produced Nat King Cole, Peggy Lee, and Frank Sinatra, called to tell me about it.

I was still having trouble speaking, so Sue answered all the phone calls. I heard her in the kitchen say, "Hi, Dave."

"I want Jim to get on the other line. I want to tell you both something." Sue called out to me to pick up the phone in my study.

"Yes?" I managed to whisper.

"Jim, this is Dave. I want you both to be the first to know. When The Lettermen contract comes up for renewal in a few weeks, we're dropping them from the label. Capitol is aware of who picked the songs, who did the vocal arranging, and who had the ideas."

Dave Cavanaugh was a very compassionate man. A couple of years after my breakdown, Sue threw me a birthday party and invited him. He brought me a beautifully carved creed of the twelve steps for Alcoholics Anonymous. The steps were about how to bring yourself back up. I hung it on the door of my studio. My problem wasn't alcohol, but this helped me deal with my depression.

It looks like when Tony got rid of me, he actually shot himself in the foot. Even though I couldn't sing, I could have continued paying for my replacement and paying Tony compensation money for me not being on the road. I also could have continued arranging and using my creativity to promote the group.

Shortly after I sold The Lettermen, Gary told me that he was worried about the future of the group. He said, "Jim, we just did our first four-hour concert without you being there to direct us. People were getting up and leaving." That was something Tony and I fought about all the time when I was in the group. Behind the scenes, we'd always argue about whether or not to go out for one more song after having had multiple standing ovations. I wanted to leave the concert at its peak. You can only have so many encores. Tony, however, wanted to keep going back out for more and more, until people started leaving. I finally got to the point where I would just walk away from Tony rather than argue with him. When I was done singing, I'd go into the dressing room and start changing, and Tony would just be screaming at my back.

CHAPTER 17:
Nobody Could Paint a Dream

One of the first jobs I ever had was working for the post office as a mailman. I was truly a letterman. It was a good government job, and I was making enough money to support myself and save a little. But let me tell you, being a mailman is no picnic.

There was this one Rottweiler on my route that was chained around the side of the house. He usually barked at me, but one day as I opened the gate and walked across the front lawn, I heard running. The dog was off his chain and heading straight for me. I was halfway between the gate and the front door. I didn't think I had a chance to make it to either one before he caught up with me. I figured I was in real trouble because he wasn't barking, just running silently—like death—as fast as he could. The ground was thundering, and I thought I was dead, but he jumped up and started licking me in the face. I patted his head and pushed him back, slipped the mail in the slot, and left, but that day I thought for sure he was going to tear me apart.

Overall, being a mailman was a pretty cushy job. All that mattered was that my route was done each day. If I could get my route done by noon, I could go to an audition and then come back and clock out with everyone else. Sometimes, if we had an early audition, Bobby, Tony, and I would literally run my mail route so I'd be done in time. I was able to go to auditions and hold down a full-time job. I made a nice living and had enough money to make demo tapes, such as I did for "Their Hearts Were Full of Spring."

After I left The Lettermen, my family and I lived for quite some time with no income. Luckily, I was not a big spender, and I had saved enough to keep us afloat for those years. During that time, I formed a record label, Eagle Records, and opened up my own music publishing company called Kelly Jeanne Music, named after our daughter. I wanted to give back to the industry that had been so generous to me. I worked with young artists to help them out. I'd make demos for them in my recording studio, and some of these kids got major label record deals. I'd give them their start just like I had been given a chance all those years ago.

At one point in my life, I thought I wanted to be a producer. After I lost my rights to The Lettermen, I produced for survival. My family wasn't making any money, and since I couldn't sing, I figured, *Why not produce?* I had acted like a producer for The Lettermen—putting the music together, choosing the songs, and figuring out the vocal pieces—so why not produce? By this time in my life, I loved working in show business. To me, producing was just another hat to wear. Besides, what was I supposed to do? Go back to being a mailman?

My first idea was to start producing young Latter-Day Saint talent. My philosophy is that a great producer does what is necessary to take a song from its infancy and make it a hit record. Even if I had to say, "I'm not very good with this particular song, so I'm going to have to bring in another producer to help me," I would get that song produced.

Being a producer is complex; it takes a lot of work. Sometimes there would be four songs recorded in a day, and all four needed different musicians. Do you know how many musicians that adds up to? I think one of the hardest things about being a producer is that you have to be nice to *everyone*. There were days when I would wake up and think, *I'm not in the mood for this. I don't have any patience left.* But as the producer, you've got to be happy because you want everyone in the studio to be happy. If a musician gives you a bad time, he's gone because he could create tension and spoil the mood of the rest of the session. The same goes for the producer.

There was also all the work I was doing outside the studio, usually at my home. My wife was occasionally irritated because I'd be trying to figure out an arrangement for a song, and dinner was on the table "getting cold," but research was important. Sometimes I wouldn't quite know how I wanted a piece to sound. Then I would hear some song on the radio and say, "That's it!" I'd run home and try to figure out how to make the song sound like that.

I did have a great time producing, and I was lucky because I had developed the skill from leading The Lettermen. I was the creative force in that group. I produced forty-six consecutive hit albums without a failure. Those albums were nicely lined up in a row, making the Top 20 in *Billboard* magazine. I had two important philosophies with The Lettermen. First, every song on an album needs to be a killer. All of our albums had twelve great songs on them, not just a couple with filler songs in between. When people bought our album, they loved the whole thing—all twelve songs.

Equally important is keeping the audience entertained while staying true to who you are. Even though we were ballad singers, we were current. Our songs stayed in the Top 20—week after week, along with all the rock 'n' roll songs—because people liked our music. We would look at the current Top 10 records in *Billboard* magazine, and if any of those songs were close to our recording style, we would make an album out of them fast enough that those Top 10 records would still be the top single records being played in the nation.

CHAPTER 18:
How Many Times I Wish I Could Tell You

Even after Charlie's death, I continued to listen to the hypnosis tape. When we stayed in hotel rooms, Sue would draw a dot on the ceiling with a marker so I had my "point" to stare at as I listened to the tape. Years later, Gary stayed in one of those hotel rooms, and the dot was still there. Whenever we remember those dots, Sue asks me, "What do you think people thought when they went to bed and saw black dots on the ceiling?"

Somewhere in the back of my mind, I kept hearing Charlie say the tape was just a Band-Aid, but it was working. I was convinced I was winning because after our big night at the Fairmont in 1969, my voice continued to get better for another four years. But then the tape wasn't enough. I couldn't hit the high notes as well, and little by little, my voice started having trouble again. The Band-Aid fell off, and my wound was exposed. Suddenly it was necessary to understand what was wrong with me.

I was angry with Charlie. He told me he knew what was wrong with me, but I had to be the one to tell him—but he wasn't here anymore! He once said, "Jim, imagine you're standing at the edge of a river, and these bodies are floating past you. You're pulling the bodies out—all of them—as they go by. Now, you can choose to do this the rest of your life, but what you need to do is go upstream and find out who's throwing the bodies in and stop them." Who *was* throwing the bodies in? I didn't find the answer to that question until twenty years later.

Eventually I learned that part of my problem had to do with my dad being this unstoppable singer. The stronger my dad sang, the more threatening he was to our family. Part of me wanted to be a strong singer like my dad, but another part of me didn't want that because I didn't like him. However, I was becoming like my dad—I just didn't realize it. The better I sang and the stronger my voice got, the more controlling I became over the group and everybody else. I was becoming like my dad: all-powerful and all-consuming. The part of me that didn't want to become like him created voice trouble that, in a sense, kept me humble. That way I couldn't be like my father.

I began to recognize my dominant behavior. I had been dominating, even in the beginning, when I put the group together. I was so afraid we weren't going to succeed that I made sure we did everything my way. Everything I did made us successful, so my dominant behavior seemed right to me. One thing I realized was that I gave ultimatums, just like my dad did. We would be in the recording studio, and when anybody wanted to do something I knew wouldn't work, I became forceful and domineering. I wanted to make sure we were successful. It's not that success is a bad thing, but I learned the hard way that success isn't everything, and nothing successful ever comes without a price.

Consciously, I wanted to be out there singing and keeping my career going, but I couldn't do it. I learned from Dr. Kardiner that the subconscious is stronger than the conscious mind. If your subconscious doesn't want to do something, you're not going to be able to do it. Your subconscious is that powerful. My subconscious didn't want to sing, and because I buried my feelings and didn't confront them, I lost my voice. Of course, I didn't realize any of this at the time. I was dominant when I had a strong voice. When I lost my voice, I became submissive. I felt better when I was in the submissive role because I wasn't like my father; when I was submissive, I was actually like my mother.

When I was a child, my mom was the saint, and my father was the mean one. My mother came to live with us for a while after her third husband died in a fire. I actually began to see her as a person, not a saint. I saw how passive-aggressive she was. I could understand how she must have enraged my father because she enraged me. It made me see my dad in a whole new light. My dad actually turned out to be the sentimental one. He was the one who kept pictures and scrapbooks of our family. I finally understood him somewhat. When I went to my dad and told him he was the root of my voice problems, he cried. When I told Dr. Kardiner this, he said I had to go back and apologize. My dad had just treated me the way his father had treated him. My dad was a changed man in the end; he'd grown calmer. Parents aren't knights, so when they fall off their white horses, it's okay. I had to reconcile with both my parents. I remembered what Dr. Kardiner told me in one of our early sessions: "There never was a parent who wasn't a child." Understanding this was huge turning point for me.

I remember my first day of school in Twin Falls, Idaho. I got sent to the principal's office for beating up a bully. I had been walking by the cafeteria on my way to class when I saw this huge guy pushing a little kid against the lockers. I couldn't stand the sight of that little kid being bullied. It reminded me of being bullied by my father. In a sense, when I ran over to save the little kid, I was trying to defend myself. I figured out that when I beat up bullies at school, I was symbolically protecting myself. My father never hit me—I never saw him hit anyone actually—but he could be mean, especially if he had been drinking. There was a lot of psychological abuse, and he yelled a lot. When I was six years old, I wrote a letter to Santa asking if he would stop Dad from being so mean to Mommy. Years later, I saw that letter in my dad's scrapbook. I couldn't believe he had kept it. I don't think my dad wanted to be mean, but he did put a lot of pressure on himself to be the best. I understood that when I grew up. I lost my voice pushing myself to be perfect.

One day I walked into Dr. Kardiner's office, and he told me about "Fibber McGee's closet" and "empty leg syndrome." Dr. Kardiner explained, "With Fibber McGee's closet, you open up this closet of yours, and all your feelings and monsters come pouring onto the floor. It's a mess. Your job, Jim, is to look at all these feelings. Pull them out, touch them, and feel them. Then put them back in the closet in order. You're going to have to get your closet in order to understand everything. You got that?" I didn't at first, but then I went to visit my dad. I told him how upset I was at him for how he treated me as a kid. This was opening the closet. Several weeks later, I flew back to Idaho and told my dad I forgave him. This was putting those feelings back in the closet. I started doing that each day, little by little, until I felt I could move on with my life.

Empty leg syndrome, however, refers to what I missed as a child. As a kid, if that leg isn't filled up, it'll never be filled up. I had to learn to live with that and move on with only one leg. I had to let go and forgive. I was the one who had to make the decision whether to sink or swim. I decided I was going to swim!

CHAPTER 19:
Let Me Love You, Baby, Let Me Love You

There's nothing quite like the feeling you get when you are told you're going to be a father. Kelly Jeanne Pike was born January 10, 1977. She was the most remarkable person I had ever laid eyes on. She was so tiny—only six pounds and eight ounces. I couldn't believe anyone could be so small. Fragile. That's one word I would use to describe her as an infant. The first time I held her, I was so nervous I was trembling, but Kelly just looked at me like she knew who I was. As she held on to my finger, she went to sleep as if she felt safe in my arms.

Gary's wife, Sharon, had their first child around the same time. I remember Sharon calling Sue to tell her she was pregnant. About six weeks later, Sue called Sharon to tell her she was pregnant too. Sue had a really good pregnancy. She was never sick. She would still go on bike rides and get on the second-story ladder to clean the windows. Sue combined the Lamaze and Bradley methods of childbirth and decided to have Kelly naturally. When it came time for Kelly to be born, Sue looked over at me and said, "It

Sue with Kelly Pike

hurts?" almost like she was surprised. I stared at her, stunned, and then replied, "Well ... what did you expect?"

Kelly seemed pretty normal when she was born. There didn't seem to be anything wrong. She started walking at the right age and talking at the right age. Then, when she was two and a half years old, it was difficult to talk to her because she was echolalic, meaning she echoed her words. For example, she'd look at me and go, "Dada, dada, dada, dada," fifty times. We couldn't stop her. Sue was at the mall one day with a few of her friends, and her friend Kathy took her aside. Kathy started crying and said, "I don't want to upset you Sue, but I think there is something wrong with Kelly." Sue started crying too and said, "I think I've known for a while." When Sue and Kelly got home, Sue told me what had happened at the mall and what Kathy had said.

I replied, "I was slow and late growing up too. I don't see why we need to bring a doctor into this."

Kelly did everything in the "normal" range, but it was in the lower end of the range. When she walked, it was at fourteen months instead of earlier like most children. When she talked, it was in complete sentences, not just a word here or there.

I finally had to accept there was something wrong and agreed to take her to see a neurologist. He gave her some tests and then told us, "We think she's aphasic." Back then, autism wasn't as well known. Aphasia affects the way a child speaks, so the doctors just assumed that was what was wrong.

Kelly started preschool at age three, and teachers put her in aphasia classes. When Kelly had learned to talk, her voice and her diction were perfect. She could say, "Daddy, ball, cat, and mouse" just as clearly as I could. But

Kelly Pike (age 3)

she started coming home from school and saying, "Do-ga," (dog) "ca-ta" (cat). That's how all the other kids in the class spoke, and that was the way the teachers were teaching them. Sue and I went to the school board and tried to talk to them, but they wouldn't listen to us. When we returned to the school board, we brought Kelly's teacher with us. She told the board, "Kelly is not aphasic and doesn't belong in my class." That got their attention, and they were finally willing to listen. Next, the school tried sending Kelly to a special education class, but she was bored with it. Her teacher said, "She's too bright for the class; she doesn't belong in it."

For a while, it seemed Kelly didn't fit in anywhere at school. Sue and I were getting frustrated that Kelly wasn't satisfactorily growing or advancing. Sue decided she was going to review every special education class in the San Fernando Valley until she found a place for our daughter. When she sat in on Mrs. Gelman's class at Carpenter Avenue Grammar School in North Hollywood, Sue felt that was the class for Kelly. Mrs. Gelman said her class was full and she couldn't take anyone else. Two days later, Sue and Kelly were at another elementary school for a special test, and Mrs. Gelman happened to be there.

Sue took Kelly over to her and said, "Mrs. Gelman, I was in your class a couple days ago. This is my daughter, Kelly."

After Mrs. Gelman talked to Kelly, she turned to Sue and said, "I want Kelly in my class. I'll see to the arrangements." She started attending Carpenter Avenue the following school year when she was in fourth grade. Kelly stayed in Mrs. Gelman's class for four years. Mrs. Gelman's class was for fourth to sixth grade, but when it came time for Kelly to move on to junior high, Mrs. Gelman and the school psychiatrist felt it would be best if Kelly stayed one more year at Carpenter Avenue.

During a parent-teacher conference, Mrs. Gelman said, "The rest of the school doesn't know what grade Kelly is in because I have the fourth, fifth, and sixth graders. Kelly doesn't care where she goes, so let's keep her one more year. Going to junior high is hard, and the kids can be mean. Emotionally, Kelly should be kept back until next year when she can handle it better."

We all agreed Kelly's staying an extra year in sixth grade would be the best thing for her. She would be more mature when she did have to make the transition to junior high. It was the best decision, as she blossomed and thrived.

Kelly has always loved music. She must have gotten that from me. In our home, she had her own little area in the kitchen where she kept her cassettes and cassette player. I think she fell in love with music because she learned how to entertain herself with it. In seventh grade, Kelly joined the choir. One day, she came home and told us that her school choir was going to be performing at Universal Studios for the Christmas program. We went, and all the kids looked really good. They sounded great. Then Kelly got up and started walking down the stairs. I was thinking, *Oh no, something's wrong. Should I get up and go to her?* But Kelly walked over to the single microphone on the lower stage and sang "Silent Night" in German. She sounded amazing. Her voice was strong and unwavering. Sue and I were both shocked. After the program, we went to Kelly and asked her, "Why didn't you tell us you were going to sing 'Silent Night' in German?" She just shrugged her shoulders and said, "I don't know. I didn't think it was a big deal."

Kelly also surprised us at her junior high school graduation. Sue and I were there with a few friends to support Kelly. The principal stood up and announced he was going to start with the honor roll students. When they said "Kelly Pike," we all nearly fell over. *Our Kelly?* I kept thinking, *Our Kelly is an honor student?* Again, when we asked her why she didn't tell us, she shrugged. We offered her a gift for being on the honor roll, and she said she wanted to see Jose Carreras at the Greek Theater. What other little girl would want to see an opera singer for her graduation present? But that was Kelly. She loved opera.

When *Phantom of the Opera* was playing, Kelly fell for Michael Crawford. A friend of mine worked in the lighting department and took us up to the lighting booth to watch the show. Kelly was fascinated being able to see the trap doors from above and watching the Phantom wait to cut the chandelier. Crawford found out how much Kelly loved the show. Not long after we saw it, a special messenger came out to the house with a poster of Crawford addressed to Kelly. It read, "To Kelly, with love, Michael Crawford." When he left the show, Crawford gave Kelly his personal poster (the one that had hung in his dressing room) and one of the leather masks he had worn during the show. Gary's wife, Sharon, made Kelly a cape, and Kelly played the Phantom for Halloween. Kelly actually performed as the Phantom in our shows a few times. She would come on in her cape and mask and sing, *"Nighttime sharpens, heightens each sensation."* Then, at the end of the performance, she would pull off her mask. The audience was leaping up and cheering. After the shows, Kelly would tell us, "I got a leaping, screaming, standing ovation."

Kelly was also excited when she got to see *Cats*. She loved watching the commercials advertising that it was coming to town. We were sitting near the front row. Kelly was waiting for the part where the big tire comes down, and the new and old cats sing and dance on it. When she finally saw the tire, she leaped up and raised her arms in a touchdown position. It was funny. She got quite a few laughs out of the audience.

Kelly Jeanne Pike

One of my favorite memories is Kelly and I singing together during a church Christmas program. We sang a duet of "You Are My Special Angel" and "You Are So Beautiful to Me."

The arrangement was wonderful; there wasn't a dry eye in the room. Normally I was the one who held the long notes, but Kelly held them this time, and I countered around the notes. Before we started, Kelly looked at me and said, "Daddy, I'm so happy Heavenly Father sent me to you, and you got to be my father." I just about choked up as I told her, "I'm so grateful Heavenly Father allowed us to be your parents." It was such a tender moment between the two of us. It was hard for me to not cry during that program. I'll never forget it.

I was afraid of being a dad. I could have repeated what my father did to me, which was a repeat of what his father did to him. Yet, even though I was scared, somewhere inside of me was a confidence that I could do this; I could be a loving father to Kelly. Maybe it was because, unlike my father, I had learned and progressed. I sought help, grudgingly at first, but nonetheless, I understood myself. That gave me the support I needed to be a different father to Kelly than my dad was to me.

After Kelly was born, I grew so much more than I had in all the time I had spent seeing Charlie and Dr. Kardiner. I'll tell you what I've learned from Kelly: everything works out in the end. Raising her was like taking little steps every day, and sometimes I had to take a couple of steps back before I could move on. It wasn't always easy raising her; there was even one time when we had to hire a behavior modification specialist to help out. There were days I didn't think Sue and I could take anymore, but we always did. Even though there were bad days, they didn't matter because the good ones were so much more frequent and wonderful. I thought losing The Lettermen was the worst thing that happened to me, but if I had still been on the road, Sue and I would have never had Kelly. All of those days Kelly managed to push all my buttons, and I was sure one of us wasn't going to live to see the next day, but we did. It was like, "Another challenge I licked!" Maybe Kelly understood I needed to be challenged. At least, that's what I like to think.

When Sue and I were first told Kelly was "retarded," I went into our bedroom and cried. I got on my knees and just prayed over and over. Suddenly, a warm feeling came over my whole body, and I started crying even harder because I knew how much I loved Kelly. I loved her more than I had the day she was born. I knew everything would work out. All

Kelly did was love us, and all she asked for in return was to be loved. I could do that. I could love her. I always have.

"What are we going to do? How is she going to react to being put in those special needs classes?" Sue asked me. She thought for a long moment and then said, "I know what we'll do. If we can give her self-esteem, then she can handle whatever comes her way. My dad used to tell me, 'You can accomplish anything you put your mind to.' That's what we're going to tell Kelly." Sue was right on.

I don't think the news about Kelly being autistic shocked Sue. She knew Kelly wasn't "retarded," and it really upset her when the doctors mentioned it. Sue always felt there was something special about our daughter. Kelly had such a wise, gentle spirit about her, so when we found out about the autism, Sue said it made sense.

I came home from work one day to find Sue crying on the couch. "What's wrong? Where's Kelly?"

"Playing in her room. Jim, I—I whacked her with my open hand. I—"

"It's all right." I sat down and grabbed her hand. "It's all right. Calm down. What happened?"

"Oh, she was acting up and really upset me. I lost my patience with her. I couldn't believe I did that. Then Kelly looked at me as if to say, 'You know better than that. Why would you do that?' Can you believe that? She's only four years old, and she knows better than I do."

Kelly always seemed to know more than either one of us did. She's brought so much joy to our lives, but we went through a phase where we couldn't take her anywhere in public without her causing trouble. She was an angel at home, but she didn't comprehend what "no" meant, and if we were in a restaurant or at the supermarket, she'd be a little stinker. So the whole family took a trip to see Dr. Ritvo, the head of the Autism Department at UCLA. Dr. Ritvo had an assistant come to our house and work with Kelly once a week with behavior modification. We also established a time-out room for Kelly.

Kelly needed to learn how to function in society, so we took her everywhere with us, but it wasn't easy punishing her. One time we were at Marie Callender's, and she started acting up. Sue took Kelly out to the car and made her sit in the backseat with the windows down while Sue stood outside telling Kelly that she could go back in when she decided to behave. Sometimes Kelly would have to be in time-out for only five minutes, sometimes twenty. For a while, Sue and I couldn't eat a meal with each other at a restaurant, or even shop in a grocery store together, because one of us always ended up taking Kelly to the car.

We kept up with the time-out rule for about a year. It was an almost everyday routine, but we were consistent. If Kelly didn't behave, she went into the time-out room. Finally, she understood us, and we understood her. She learned how to behave in public, and we learned the reason she acted up was because some autistic people have a hard time filtering sound, movements, and light.

When Kelly was in high school, the big Northridge earthquake struck. That devastated her—it rocked her world. The books in her bookcase came crashing down in her bedroom, and we couldn't get her bedroom door to open. She was scared to death, so much so that she couldn't function. She was traumatized for six months, which made going to school really hard on her. This happened close to when she was graduating. She got better, and everything was fine once we got her on medication. It just took awhile for the shock from the earthquake to die down.

Kelly was about to graduate when her doctor told us, "Kelly has to live on her own."

I asked him, "Who can love her and take care of her as well as we can?"

His answer surprised me. "Nobody, but she has to have her own life. You're not going to be around forever."

That shook me a bit. Sue and I talked to Kelly's teacher at school, and she told us about an independent living program. Kelly was disappointed because all her friends at church and school were going off to college. She wanted to know why she wasn't going off to school. One of the ladies in our church, who knew about the situation, said, "Kelly is going to go away to independent living like other kids go to college, and she's going to go into work training for college." This lady offered to give Kelly a going-away party if she could use our backyard for it. There must have been over one hundred people at the party. It was a really kind thing for that woman to do for Kelly. Kelly has always been liked by others.

After graduation, Kelly moved into the Community Independent Living Program (CLIP) in Woodland Hills, California, at the Oakwood apartments. When we got ready to move Kelly into her apartment, the staff said to Sue, "Now, Sue, when Kelly comes down here, it's usually harder on the moms than the dads. You're not going to be able to talk to Kelly for a month because she has to break the apron strings and get used to not having you around." The day we moved Kelly out there, Sue had these cute little pictures to hang on the walls along with a quilted fabric hanging with family snapshots on it. We lined Kelly's shelves, and we got her towels and bed linens to match. Her bedroom was adorable, and she was situated. When it was time to go, Sue and I walked out to the car while Kelly stood there in the parking lot, smiling and waving good-bye. We lost it as we drove home. I had to pull over until we were done crying and I was able to see the road clearly.

A week later, the head of the staff unexpectedly called us and said, "Kelly's just fine. You can call her any time you want. She feels good about herself."

The older Kelly becomes, the more fun she is to be with. She no longer gets upset or yells when she gets stressed. With each passing year, she's become more and more mellow. Now we can go places and do things with her. We know she's ready to see us when she calls and says, "I haven't seen you for a while." She will even call and say, "I haven't been on an airplane in a while." She's hinting that she's ready to go with us to our next concert.

We worked very hard with Kelly. We have dedicated ourselves to her. I was her playmate and friend, not just her father. I would drop everything for Kelly; she's my greatest production.

CHAPTER 20:
Put Your Head on My Shoulder

Losing my voice prepared me for the other hardships I would face in my life. We moved to Big Bear, California, in 1998. It was a hectic time. Sue and I had lived in Toluca Lake for over thirty years. We packed everything in ninety days and moved it all to Big Bear. We both had been so busy that we were overdue by six months for our yearly physicals. Sue was anxious to get our physicals scheduled because several of my friends had had prostate problems. Sue called to make the appointments. While she was at hers, Sue's doctor discovered a lump but didn't tell her. The doctor just said, "Sue, while you're down from the mountain, why don't you have a mammogram? I'll set it up right now." I sat in the office waiting while Sue had the mammogram. When I saw the doctor walk in and out a few times, I knew something was up. She was having an ultrasound when Sue's doctor called and said, "Sue, it's highly suspected that you have breast cancer." I drove her to get a biopsy the next day, which was a Thursday.

The doctor called us on Saturday and said, "I have good news and bad news."

"We all know what the bad news is," Sue said.

"Yes, but the good news is your tumor margins are clean."

But that really wasn't the good news. They thought the margins were clean, but the cancer had already gotten into the bloodstream and into Sue's lymph nodes. Sue had a mastectomy where they removed eleven lymph nodes. Out of the eleven, three were infected. If they hadn't removed them, Sue would be dead now. Isn't it interesting that Sue was worried about me and got the appointments for our physicals, and it ended up saving her life.

I drove Sue to Los Angeles for every chemotherapy appointment and sat by her side. Most of the time, however, she would call one of my friends and tell them, "Go meet Jim for lunch." It was just like her to be worrying about me eating, when she was the one going through chemo.

After the mastectomy, Sue went through reconstructive surgery. Her doctor, Dr. Kulber, told Sue she was going to feel like she'd been hit by a Mack truck. After the surgery, while in recovery, Sue asked him, "Dr. Kulber, how many Mack trucks?"

That surgery was followed by more chemo and radiation. Sue did really well and healed very quickly, but it was hard. One morning, I was in the bathroom with Sue measuring the drainage from the tubes she had in her. Suddenly, she sank to her knees on the tile and started crying and said, "I'm sorry I'm not beautiful. I have all these scars."

I started crying, looked at her, and said, "Honey, you're more beautiful to me now than ever. Don't you know how good it makes me feel to finally take care of you? You always supported me and went through so much for me. Don't you realize how much I love being able to do something for you?"

Sue had always taken care of me and everyone else in her life; she was the strong one. I hated seeing her in so much pain, but I was grateful that she didn't have to go through the pain alone because I would never leave her side. It was a comfort to me, during this time of uncertainty, to know we would be together for all eternity.

Jim and Sue Pike

CHAPTER 21:
I Made It through the Rain

Just a few weeks after I came home from Edgemont hospital, I was talking to a friend, Ed Cobb, who was the bass singer for The Four Preps. I was over at his house when I told him what I had gone through and what my psychiatrists had done for me. Then, as I whispered, "I'm afraid of DEATH," my voice opened up—clear as a bell—as if nothing had ever happened. I started crying and dancing around the room. It lasted for about fifteen minutes, and then my voice closed back up. My voice didn't open up again until six months later, this time for thirty minutes. For a year, it was like a roller coaster. I would be whispering and something inside of me would let go. My voice would open up, and then it would close up again.

My voice got stronger and stronger over the next couple of years to the point where I might only lose my voice once a week. I was so grateful for the moments I could talk to Sue and Kelly and tell them how much I loved them without having to write it down on paper. Every once in a while, I would say something, and my voice would become unusually loud like a radio announcer, and then it would quiet back down to a normal tone. The more I started talking, the easier it became. Then one day, I realized my singing voice was back too. I thought my depression was finally over and all my troubles were behind me.

Well, nothing ever really works out that simply. Around 1990, Dr. Kardiner diagnosed me with clinical depression and prescribed an anti-depressant. Even though I had to deal with depression, my voice was strong once more. I was speaking and singing again and loving every minute of it. Early each morning, I would slowly count to twenty and then say the alphabet. I continued doing this as a voice exercise for many years.

One day, I got a phone call from Bobby Engemann. Bobby was singing in a group called Star with his boss and his boss's two daughters. They were doing The Lettermen shows under the title "Tribute to The Lettermen" and were singing all of our hits. Bobby asked if I would come up to Salt Lake for a concert they were going to do in Symphony Hall.

"I don't know about that, Bobby."

"Just sit incognito in the audience. That's all I'm asking. If you're okay with it, one of our girls, Tammy, will come down and sit on your lap. She'll grab your hand and bring you up onstage. Then you sing."

Monday, Nove:

Ex-Letterman regains voice and career

By REX RUTKOSKI
Staff Writer

MONROEVILLE — Jim Pike is translating 13 years of musical frustration into a rebirth of his career.

The former leader of the Lettermen left the stage several years ago, his doctors telling him he would never sing again.

For two years, he even lost his

Nightclub Review

speaking voice and was forced to write notes to his wife.

Pike began having throat problems from the first day he started singing professionally, and he experienced a slow, gradual decline for 13 years.

Eagle Records Co.

Jim Pike

Article in the Enquirer

He talked me into it, and a few days later, I found myself on a flight to Salt Lake. I was scared out of my mind. How long had it been since I had sung in front of a live audience? Sue kept reminding me there would be five other voices up there that would cover for me if my voice wasn't strong enough. So I went, and in the middle of a number, Tammy came down and pulled me up onstage. The audience—went—wild! *Everybody* recognized me. They were screaming and throwing cushions in the air! Then we started singing the hits medley, and I could sing! I was really close to the microphone, singing softly because I was nervous, but when the audience started shouting because they saw Bobby and me together, I let my voice get a little louder. After the show, Bobby and I ran offstage and flew into each other's arms—just like Gary and I did when my voice came back for the first time. We were crying. The kids were crying. Everyone kept saying to Bobby, "You and Jim have to do this again." It was 1983, and Reunion was born.

Ric de Azevedo, Jim Pike, Bobby Engemann (Reunion)

Reunion started with me, Bobby, and Ric de Azevedo, one of the King Family who sang on television. Ric's mother, Alyce Clark, was a

King sister. Bobby and I had seen Ric in the musical *Saturday's Warrior* and knew we wanted him to sing with us. On our first poster of Reunion, Ric had a mustache, but no one liked it because The Lettermen had been clean-shaven, so he shaved his off.

The name Reunion came pretty easily. It was still a kind of collegiate name, and since we were reuniting two-thirds of the original Lettermen, it fit. We weren't sure people would be interested in Reunion, but when they realized it had two of the original Lettermen in it, we started making some noise. I'd go out onstage and be introduced as "Jim Pike of the original Lettermen."

I worked on my voice for almost an entire year, and it paid off. The first time I made it through a whole show since losing my voice was May 1983. It was at a big Amway convention in New Orleans. Dan Williams called and wanted us to sing for them. We were all nervous about doing our first show. In rehearsal, I belted out a mighty tone. I knew I could do it. We sang Neil Diamond's "Coming to America" as our opener. The audience loved it because that song is about a jazz singer coming on a boat to America, and New Orleans was the birthplace of jazz. We received a standing ovation after every single song that night. What did we have to worry about? It seemed like the public was ready for Reunion. Personally, I think we sounded better than when we were The Lettermen.

Bobby, Ric, and I were Reunion until 1999. Bobby had been sick for a couple of years when he told me he couldn't do it anymore. I wasn't going to ask him to leave; he had to tell me when he was ready. Maybe Bobby risked it a bit. At one point, his illness got so bad that we were taking Bobby to the emergency room after every concert because we were afraid he was going to die. Still, I waited until Bobby told me he had to leave because I couldn't bear to kick him out the way Tony had kicked me out of The Lettermen. For the second time in my singing career, I replaced Bobby with my brother Gary.

Sue has been a huge help with Reunion. When our group first got together, Arthur Silver was our road manager. After he left, rather than hiring someone else, I told Sue, "You know you can do this. Why don't *you* be our road manager? That way, you'll get to go with us."

She was hesitant at first. "I don't know. When you were in The Lettermen, I was just a wife. I pressed your suit, I'd answer fan mail, but I really didn't have anything to do with the actual group. You really think I can do this?"

Ric de Azevedo, Jim Pike, Gary Pike (Reunion)

"I know you can."

Sue is amazing; she's our needle and thread. Whatever needs to be done, Sue can handle it. She really took being our road manager to heart. She's very organized and has a stack of papers with her all the time: a sheet she composed for the sound rider, lighting cues, contracts, room assignments at the hotels, intro sheets, etc., etc., etc. Sue didn't know what to do at first, but she learned very quickly and does an excellent job. It wasn't long after Sue started that she was giving sound and lighting cues. She makes me laugh when people ask her what she does. "I'm the den mother," she says. "It's me and seven guys." Honestly, she's great. She takes care of all the last-minute details. Anything that comes up, she's on top of it. Sue's also good with the bookkeeping (something I've never been too fond of doing) and payroll and taxes. A doctor once told me, "You have a tough wife!" I nodded at him and said, "You bet I do."

About ten years ago, Reunion did a concert for the governor of Idaho. We had done a show at Boise State University, and Governor Kempthorne saw us and flipped. He said he couldn't wait for us to come back. We gave him one of our cards and some CDs. About a year later, he called from the hospital where he had just had back surgery. He wanted to invite us to a celebration they do every five years honoring people who have come from Idaho and have made a name for themselves. He wanted Reunion to be a part of it. When we were there, we were presented with a beautiful gold medallion. Governor Kempthorne also asked us to be the entertainment at the Western Governors Association in Coeur d'Alene, Idaho. That was one of the most secured places I've ever been because they were expecting President George W. Bush to attend. Every time we entered the building, there were guard dogs, and we had to carry around these huge passes to get through any doors. After our performance, the governor of Montana came up to us and said, "When Montana is in charge of this, I've got to have you." And they did. Everyone wanted Reunion back.

EPILOGUE:
Life Is Still Worthwhile If You Just Smile

Happiness comes from within. I have learned that things happen for a reason. If I hadn't lost my voice, Sue and I would have been on the road for a long time. We probably wouldn't have had Kelly or a normal life. We all have been given trials to help us grow. I know losing my voice was one of those trials. We have to make the choice to move past our hardships or let them knock

Jim Pike

us off our feet. When we handle setbacks, we get stronger. I've grown closer to myself, my wife, my daughter, and God. I realize the more I do for someone else, the more I am able to love life.

Over the past fifty years as a performer, I've learned a few things. First, by bringing pleasure to the audience, that joy was returned to me.

The second is about friends. I have formed many long-lasting friendships. People who have been there for me, through the good times and the hard times, are truly friends.

Third is being thankful for the experiences and opportunities I was allowed to have, such as being in the Rose Garden at the White House and meeting President Reagan. In Japan, I got to go to places normal tourists don't get to see. The TV shows I was able to perform on and the celebrities I met who became friends all mean so much to me.

I still get hoarse after we've done a concert, but my voice is okay. I don't have to strain it. I think I've worked through my big problems. There will be times when I'm speaking and I still hold back. Dr. Kardiner feels it's just a habit for me now. When something comes up that I'm afraid of or don't want to deal with, my voice tightens up. I practice stopping, taking a deep breath, regaining composure, and putting myself back in control, so if my voice tries to close up, I can stop it. Thanks to The Lettermen, Reunion, my education, and all my experiences, I'm better now than where I came from. I know that with my wife, my family, friends, and God on my side, there isn't anything I can't accomplish. Anyone can overcome life's obstacles if they stick with what they believe in, have faith in themselves, and never give up. Let the music keep playing—I'm still here.

Jim Pike

DISCOGRAPHY

Jim, Tony And Bob ◄ (2 versions)	Capitol Records	1962
Once Upon A Time (LP)	Capitol Records	1962
A Song For Young Love ◄ (2 versions)	Capitol Records	1963
A Lettermen Kind Of Love (LP)	Capitol Records	1963
Look At Love (LP, Album)	Capitol Records	1964
She Cried (LP)	Capitol Records	1964
Portrait Of My Love ◄ (2 versions)	Capitol Records	1965
You'll Never Walk Alone ◄ (2 versions)	Capitol Records	1965
More Hit Sounds Of The Lettermen! ◄ (2 versions)	Capitol Records	1966
For Christmas This Year ◄ (2 versions)	Capitol Records	1966
Warm ◄ (2 versions)	Capitol Records	1967
The Lettermen!!! ... And "Live!" (LP)	Capitol Records	1967
Spring! (LP)	Capitol Records	1967
Special Request (LP)	Capitol Records	1968
Love Letters (2xLP)	Capitol Records	1968
Put Your Head On My Shoulder (LP)	Capitol Records	1968
Hurt So Bad ◄ (2 versions)	Capitol Records	1969
I Have Dreamed (8-Trk, Album)	Capitol Records	1969
Reflections ◄ (2 versions)	Capitol Records	1970
Feelings (LP)	Capitol Records	1971
Everything's Good About You (LP, Album)	Capitol Records	1971
Love Book (LP)	Capitol Records	1971
Spin Away (LP, Album)	Capitol Records	1972
"Alive" Again ... Naturally (LP, Album)	Capitol Records	1973
Make A Time For Lovin' (LP)	Capitol Records	1973
Now And Forever (LP, Album)	Capitol Records, Capitol Records	1974

	The Magic Sound / Two Hearts (7")	Warner Bros. Records	1960
	When I Fall in Love / Smile ◄ (3 versions)	Capitol Records	1961
	The Way You Look Tonight / That's My Desire ◄ (2 versions)	Capitol Records	1961
	Turn Around Look At Me / How Is Julie? ◄ (2 versions)	Capitol Records	1962
	Come Back Silly Girl (7", Single)	Capitol Records	1962
	Silly Boy (She Doesn't Love You) / I Told The Stars (7")	Capitol Records	1962
	Theme From "A Summer Place" / Sealed With A Kiss (7", Single)	Capitol Records	1965
	The Things We Did Last Summer / Secretly (7")	Capitol Records	1965
	Love Letters (7")	Capitol Records	1966
	I Believe / Sweet September (7", Single)	Capitol Records	1967
	Volare (7", Promo)	Capitol Records	1967
	I Believe // Goin' Out Of My Head / Can't Take My Eyes Off Of You (7", Single)	Capitol Records	1967
	Love Is Blue / Greensleeves (Medley) (7")	Capitol Records	1968
	Sherry Don't Go (7")	Capitol Records	1968
	Put Your Head On My Shoulder / Mary's Rainbow (7")	Capitol Records	1968
	Traces / Memories Medley (7")	Capitol Records	1969
	When Summer Ends / Shangri-La (7")	Capitol Records	1969
	Hurt So Bad / Catch The Wind (7")	Capitol Records	1969
	For Love / She Cried (7")	Capitol Records	1970
	Hey, Girl / Worlds (7", Single)	Capitol Records	1970
	Love	Capitol Records	1971
	Everything Is Good About You / It's Over (7")	Capitol Records	1971
	An Old Fashioned Love Song (7")	Capitol Records	1972
	Mac Arthur Park / Summer Song (7")	Capitol Records	1973

CDs by REUNION

REUNION—*The Greatest Hits*

REUNION—*I Believe*

REUNION—*Alive Again*

REUNION—*Jim Pike, The Solos*

REUNION—*The Songs We Sang for You*

REUNION—*It Must Be Love*

reunion@jimpike.net

ABOUT THE AUTHOR

After living in the heart of Hollywood for twenty-five years, Jim and Sue Pike decided to move to the quiet solitude of Big Bear Lake, California. There they enjoyed fishing and boating, the beauties of nature, and entertaining their numerous friends from all over the world. Following several harsh winters, they opted for a more moderate climate in the desert. Jim enjoys bowling, golfing, and playing tennis. He loves spending time with his daughter, Kelly, the love of his life. When he performs today, he still gets the same thrill as when he heard the song from his first hit record being played on the radio, back in August 1961—"The Way You Look Tonight."